Cambridge
IGCSE®

# Computer Science

ENDORSED BY

International Examinations

# Cambridge
# IGCSE®

# Computer
# Science

David Watson
Helen Williams

HODDER
EDUCATION
AN HACHETTE UK COMPANY

## Acknowledgements

Computer hardware and software brand names mentioned in this book are protected by their respective trademarks and are acknowledged.

Scratch is developed by the Lifelong Kindergarten Group at the MIT Media Lab. See http://scratch.mit.edu

Every effort have been made to trace all copyright holders, but if any have been inadvertently overlooked the publishers will be pleased to make the necessary arrangements at the first opportunity.

Although every effort has been made to ensure that website addresses are correct at time of going to press, Hodder Education cannot be held responsible for the content of any website mentioned in this book. It is sometimes possible to find a relocated web page by typing in the address of the home page for a website in the URL window of your browser.

## Photo credits

**p.1** © peno – Fotolia; **p.15** © Dmitrydesigner/Fotolia; **p.16** ©iStockphoto.com/Karl Yamashita; **p.57** © Romanchuck – Fotolia; **p.58** *t* © C Squared Studios/Photodisc/Getty Images, *m* ©Dmitriy Melnikov - Fotolia.com, *b* © Popova Olga/Fotolia; **p.59** © picsfive – Fotolia; **p.65** © Manfred Schmidt – Fotolia.com; **p.67** © dja65 – Fotolia; **p.68** © Konstantin Shevtsov – Fotolia; **p.69** *t* © Miguel Navarro/Stone/Getty Images, *b* © Piero Cruciatti/Alamy; **p.73** © Jamdesign/Fotolia; **p.78 and 79** © adisa – Fotolia; **p.81** © Mykola Mazuryk – Fotolia; **p.82** *t* © Mauro Rodrigues/Fotolia, *b* ©Martin Dohrn/Science Photo Library; **p.83** © Norman Chan – Fotolia; **p.85** © Studio 10 /Alamy; **p.86** © Brennan JB7 produced by Martin Brennan; **p.87** © Sergojpg/Fotolia; **p.88 and 110** *b* © Jürgen Fälchle/Fotolia; **p.108** *t* © Andrew Brown/Fotolia, *b* © Stanford Eye Clinic/Science Photo Library; **p.114** © Tan Kian Khoon – Fotolia.

*t* = top, *b* = bottom, *l* = left, *r* = right, *c* = centre

Hachette UK's policy is to use papers that are natural, renewable and recyclable products and made from wood grown in sustainable forests. The logging and manufacturing processes are expected to conform to the environmental regulations of the country of origin.

Orders: please contact Bookpoint Ltd, 130 Milton Park, Abingdon, Oxon OX14 4SB. Telephone: (44) 01235 827720. Fax: (44) 01235 400454. Lines are open 9.00–5.00, Monday to Saturday, with a 24-hour message answering service. Visit our website at www.hoddereducation.com

® IGCSE is the registered trademark of Cambridge Assessment International Education

© David Watson and Helen Williams 2015
First published in 2015 by
Hodder Education
An Hachette UK Company
Carmelite House, 50 Victoria Embankment, London EC4Y 0DZ

Impression number  8

Year   2018

Cover photo © Scanrail – Fotolia

Third edition typeset in 11/13 pt Galliard Roman by Aptara Inc.

Printed in Dubai

A catalogue record for this title is available from the British Library

**ISBN 978 1471809309**

# Contents

# Introduction

## Aims

This textbook has been written to provide the knowledge, understanding and practical skills that a student would need for the *Cambridge Assessment International Education Computer Science IGCSE* and *GCE O Level* courses.

The textbook is part of a package which includes online material. A teacher's CD-ROM is also available separately which includes additional guidance and other useful information (see later in this introduction).

This book and accompanying online material provide:

- practice end-of-chapter questions which include questions from past *Cambridge International* papers
- activities which give students additional guidance and practice
- sample program solutions for programming activities
- hints and tips where these provide additional help and knowledge.

Although this book has been written with the *Cambridge International* syllabus in mind, it can still be used as a useful reference textbook for other GCSE computing courses. It is also a useful source of information for those students starting an A level computer science course – especially at AS level.

## Using the book

The textbook contains 13 chapters. Although it is possible for some elements of the practical problem-solving chapters to be examined in Paper 1 (Theory of Computer Science), and vice versa, the sections for the theory work are in Chapters 1 to 8 and the practical work in Chapters 9 to 13. The book has been split into Section 1 (Theory of computer science) and Section 2 (Practical problem-solving and programming) to follow the *Cambridge International* syllabus as closely as possible.

Activities are shown throughout the books as follows:

**Activity 1.1**

## Online material

The accompanying online material contains additional guidance to enhance the learning process in a number of key areas in the textbook. The online material uses animation and verbal commentary wherever this is found helpful in the learning process. The online material includes sample program solutions for the programming activities.

Where book topics are included in the online material the following symbol is used:

## Teacher's CD-ROM

An additional teacher's CD-ROM is available to accompany this textbook. This CD-ROM includes the following material:

- possible responses to sample examination and other questions
- each question part suggests a level of difficulty
- expected responses to the questions at that level are included
- additional notes on why the responses meet the required level only

- answers to the end-of-chapter questions in this textbook and to some of the activities where relevant
- program files in Python and Java for activities and end-of-chapter questions.
- a scheme of work to help teacher's plan their two-year computer science course; this scheme includes:
  - chapter numbers from the book
  - topic to be covered from the chapter
  - approximate time allocation advised to cover the topic
  - *Cambridge International* syllabus reference
  - relevant page numbers from the textbook
  - activities found in the textbook to help in the teaching process
  - any additional notes to help plan the lessons.

The teacher's CD-ROM has not been through the Cambridge endorsement process.

*David Watson and Helen Williams*

# Section 1

# Theory of computer science

**Chapters**

# 1 Binary systems and hexadecimal

> In this chapter you will learn about:
>
> ● the binary system
> ● measurement of computer memories
> ● the hexadecimal system
> ● how to convert numbers between different number base systems

## 1.1 Introduction

As you progress through this book you will begin to realise how complex computer systems really are. By the time you reach Chapter 12 you should have a better understanding of the fundamentals behind computers themselves and the software that controls them.

However, no matter how complex the system, the basic building block in all computers is the binary number system. This system is chosen since it consists of 1s and 0s only. Since computers contain millions and millions of tiny 'switches', which must be in the ON or OFF position, this lends itself logically to the binary system. A switch in the ON position can be represented by 1; a switch in the OFF position can be represented by 0.

## 1.2 The binary system

We are all familiar with the denary (base 10) number system which counts in multiples of 10. This gives us the well-known place values of units, 10s, 100s, 1000s and so on:

| 10 000 | 1000 | 100 | 10 | 1 |
|--------|------|-----|-----|-----|
| $(10^4)$ | $(10^3)$ | $(10^2)$ | $(10^1)$ | $(10^0)$ |

The BINARY SYSTEM is based on the number 2. Thus, only the two 'values' 0 and 1 can be used in this system to represent each digit. Using the same method as denary, this gives the headings of $2^0$, $2^1$, $2^2$, $2^3$ and so on. The typical headings for a binary number with eight digits would be:

| 128 | 64 | 32 | 16 | 8 | 4 | 2 | 1 |
|-----|-----|-----|-----|-----|-----|-----|-----|
| $(2^7)$ | $(2^6)$ | $(2^5)$ | $(2^4)$ | $(2^3)$ | $(2^2)$ | $(2^1)$ | $(2^0)$ |

A typical binary number would be:

1 1 1 0 1 1 1 0

## 1.2.1 Converting from binary to denary

It is fairly straightforward to change a binary number into a denary number. Each time a 1 appears in a column, the column value is added to the total. For example, the binary number above is:

128 + 64 + 32 + 8 + 4 + 2 = 238 (denary)

The 0 values are simply ignored.

## Activity 1.1

Convert the following binary numbers
into denary:

a 0 0 1 1 0 0 1 1
b 0 1 1 1 1 1 1 1
c 1 0 0 1 1 0 0 1
d 0 1 1 1 0 1 0 0
e 1 1 1 1 1 1 1 1
f 0 0 0 0 1 1 1 1
g 1 0 0 0 1 1 1 1
h 1 1 1 1 0 0 0 0
i 0 1 1 1 0 0 0 0
j 1 1 1 0 1 1 1 0

## 1.2.2 Converting from denary to binary

The reverse operation, converting from denary to binary, is slightly more
complex. There are two basic ways of doing this.

**Method 1**

Consider the conversion of the denary number, 107, into binary. This method
involves placing 1s in the appropriate position so that the total equates to 107:

| 128 | 64 | 32 | 16 | 8 | 4 | 2 | 1 |
|-----|----|----|----|---|---|---|---|
| 0   | 1  | 1  | 0  | 1 | 0 | 1 | 1 |

**Method 2**

This method involves successive division by 2. The remainders are then read from
BOTTOM to TOP to give the binary value. Again using 107, we get:

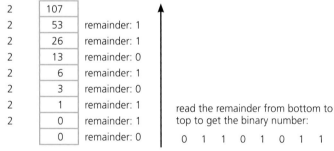

read the remainder from bottom to
top to get the binary number:

0  1  1  0  1  0  1  1

**Figure 1.1**

## Activity 1.2

Convert the following denary numbers into
binary (using both methods):

a 4 1
b 6 7
c 8 6
d 1 0 0
e 1 1 1
f 1 2 7
g 1 4 4
h 1 8 9
i 2 0 0
j 2 5 5

## 1.3   Measurement of the size of computer memories

A **b**inary dig**it** is commonly referred to as a BIT; 8 bits are usually referred to as a BYTE.

The byte is the smallest unit of memory in a computer. Some computers use larger bytes but they are always multiples of 8 (e.g. 16-bit systems and 32-bit systems). One byte of memory wouldn't allow you to store very much information; therefore memory size is measured in the following multiples:

**Table 1.1**

| Name of memory size | Number of bits | Equivalent denary value |
|---|---|---|
| 1 kilobyte (1 KB) | $2^{10}$ | 1 024 bytes |
| 1 megabyte (1 MB) | $2^{20}$ | 1 048 576 bytes |
| 1 gigabyte (1 GB) | $2^{30}$ | 1 073 741 824 bytes |
| 1 terabyte (1 TB) | $2^{40}$ | 1 099 511 627 776 bytes |
| 1 petabyte (1 PB) | $2^{50}$ | 1 125 899 906 842 624 bytes |

(Note: $1024 \times 1024 = 1\,048\,576$ and so on.)

To give some idea of the scale of these numbers, a typical data transfer rate using the internet is 32 megabits (i.e. 4 MB) per second (so a 40 MB file would take 10 seconds to transfer). Most hard disk systems in computers are 1 or 2 TB in size (so a 2 TB memory could store over half a million 4 MB photos, for example).

It should be pointed out here that there is some confusion in the naming of memory sizes. The IEC convention is now adopted by some organisations. Manufacturers of storage devices often use the denary system to measure storage size. For example,

1 kilobyte = 1000 byte

1 megabyte = 1 000 000 bytes

1 gigabyte = 1 000 000 000 bytes

1 terabyte = 1 000 000 000 000 bytes and so on.

The IEC convention for computer internal memories (including RAM) becomes:

1 kibibyte (1 KiB) = 1024 bytes

1 mebibyte (1 MiB) = 1 048 576 bytes

1 gibibyte (1 GiB) = 1 073 741 824 bytes

1 tebibyte (1 TiB) = 1 099 511 627 776 bytes and so on.

However, the IEC terms are not universally used and this textbook will use the more conventional terms shown in Table 1.1. This also ties up with the Cambridge International Examinations computer science syllabus which uses the same terminology as in Table 1.1.

## 1.4   Example use of binary

This section gives an example of a use of the binary system. We will introduce the idea of computer REGISTERS; this subject is covered in more depth in Chapter 4. A register is a group of bits; it is often depicted as follows:

| 1 | 0 | 0 | 1 | 0 | 1 | 1 | 1 |

**Figure 1.2**

When computers (or microprocessors) are used to control devices (such as robots), registers are used as part of the control system. The following example describes how registers can be used in controlling a simple device.

A robot vacuum cleaner has three wheels, A, B and C. A rotates on a spindle to allow for direction changes (as well as forward and backward movement); B and C are fixed to revolve around their axles to provide *only* forward and backward movement, and have an electric motor attached:

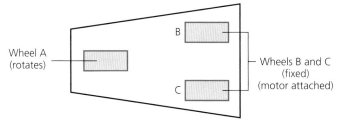

**Figure 1.3**

An 8-bit register is used to control the movement of the robot vacuum cleaner:

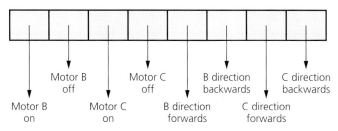

**Figure 1.4**

If the register contains 1 0 1 0 1 0 1 0 this means *'motor B is ON and motor C is ON and both motors are turning to produce FORWARDS motion'*. Effectively, the vacuum cleaner is moving forwards.

> ## Activity 1.3
> a What would be the effect if the register contained the following values?
>   i  1 0 0 1 1 0 0 0
>   ii  1 0 1 0 0 1 0 1
>   iii  1 0 1 0 0 1 1 0
> b What would the register contain if only motor C was ON and the motors were turning in a BACKWARDS direction?
> c What would the register contain if motor B and motor C were both ON but B was turning in a backward direction and C was turning in a forward direction?
> d What would be the effect if the register contained the following?
>   1 1 1 1 1 1 1 1

## 1.5 The hexadecimal system

The HEXADECIMAL SYSTEM is very closely related to the binary system. Hexadecimal (sometimes referred to as simply 'hex') is a base 16 system and therefore needs to use 16 different 'values' to represent each digit.

Because it is a system based on 16 different digits, the numbers 0 to 9 and the letters A to F are used to represent each hexadecimal (hex) digit. (A = 10, B = 11, C = 12, D = 13, E = 14 and F = 15.) Using the same method as denary and binary, this gives the headings of $16^0$, $16^1$, $16^2$, $16^3$ and so on. The typical headings for a hexadecimal number with five digits would be:

| 65 536 | 4 096 | 256 | 16 | 1 |
|--------|-------|-----|----|----|
| $(16^4)$ | $(16^3)$ | $(16^2)$ | $(16^1)$ | $(16^0)$ |

Since $16 = 2^4$ this means that FOUR binary digits are equivalent to each hexadecimal digit. Table 1.2 summarises the link between binary, hexadecimal and denary.

**Table 1.2**

| Binary value | Hexadecimal value | Denary value |
|--------------|-------------------|--------------|
| 0 0 0 0 | 0 | 0 |
| 0 0 0 1 | 1 | 1 |
| 0 0 1 0 | 2 | 2 |
| 0 0 1 1 | 3 | 3 |
| 0 1 0 0 | 4 | 4 |
| 0 1 0 1 | 5 | 5 |
| 0 1 1 0 | 6 | 6 |
| 0 1 1 1 | 7 | 7 |
| 1 0 0 0 | 8 | 8 |
| 1 0 0 1 | 9 | 9 |
| 1 0 1 0 | A | 10 |
| 1 0 1 1 | B | 11 |
| 1 1 0 0 | C | 12 |
| 1 1 0 1 | D | 13 |
| 1 1 1 0 | E | 14 |
| 1 1 1 1 | F | 15 |

## 1.5.1 Converting from binary to hexadecimal and from hexadecimal to binary

Converting from binary to hexadecimal is a fairly easy process. Starting from the right and moving left, split the binary number into groups of 4 bits. If the last group has less than 4 bits, then simply fill in with 0s from the left. Take each group of 4 bits and convert it into the equivalent hexadecimal digit using Table 1.2. Look at the following two examples to see how this works.

## Example 1

1 0 1 1 1 1 1 0 0 0 0 1

First split this up into groups of 4 bits:

1 0 1 1   1 1 1 0   0 0 0 1

Then, using Table 1.2, find the equivalent hexadecimal digits:

B        E        1

## Example 2

1 0 0 0 0 1 1 1 1 1 1 1 0 1

First split this up into groups of 4 bits:

> 1 0   0 0 0 1   1 1 1 1   1 1 0 1

The left group only contains 2 bits, so add in two 0s:

> **0 0** 1 0   0 0 0 1   1 1 1 1   1 1 0 1

Now use Table 1.2 to find the equivalent hexadecimal digits:

> 2         1         F         D

---

## Activity 1.4

Convert the following binary numbers
into hexadecimal:

a 1 1 0 0 0 0 1 1
b 1 1 1 1 0 1 1 1
c 1 0 0 1 1 1 1 1 1 1
d 1 0 0 1 1 1 0 1 1 1 0
e 0 0 0 1 1 1 1 0 0 0 0 1
f 1 0 0 0 1 0 0 1 1 1 1 0
g 0 0 1 0 0 1 1 1 1 1 1 1 0
h 0 1 1 1 0 1 0 0 1 1 1 0 0
i 1 1 1 1 1 1 1 1 0 1 1 1 1 1 0 1
j 0 0 1 1 0 0 1 1 1 1 0 1 0 1 1 1 0

---

Converting from hexadecimal to binary is also very straightforward. Using the data in Table 1.2, simply take each hexadecimal digit and write down the 4-bit code which corresponds to the digit.

# Example 3

> 4         5         A

Using Table 1.2, find the 4-bit code for each digit:

> 0 1 0 0   0 1 0 1   1 0 1 0

Put the groups together to form the binary number:

> 0 1 0 0 0 1 0 1 1 0 1 0

# Example 4

> B         F         0         8

Again just use Table 1.2:

> 1 0 1 1   1 1 1 1   0 0 0 0   1 0 0 0

Then put all the digits together:

> 1 0 1 1 1 1 1 1 0 0 0 0 1 0 0 0

---

## Activity 1.5

Convert the following hexadecimal numbers into binary:

| | |
|---|---|
| a 6 C | f B A 6 |
| b 5 9 | g 9 C C |
| c A A | h 4 0 A A |
| d A 0 0 | i D A 4 7 |
| e 4 0 E | j 1 A B 0 |

---

## 1.5.2 Converting from hexadecimal to denary and from denary to hexadecimal

To convert a hexadecimal number to denary is fairly straightforward. Take each hexadecimal digit and multiply it by its value. Add the totals together to obtain the denary value.

### Example 1

| 4 | 5 | A |

First multiply each digit by its value:

| 256 | 16 | 1 |
| (4 × 256 = 1024) | (5 × 16 = 80) | (10 × 1 = 10)   (Note: A = 10) |

Add the totals together:

denary number = 1 1 1 4

### Example 2

| C | 8 | F |

First multiply each digit by its value:

| 256 | 16 | 1 |
| (12 × 256 = 3072) | (8 × 16 = 128) | (15 × 1 = 15)   (Note: C = 12 and F = 15) |

Add the totals together:

denary number = 3 2 1 5

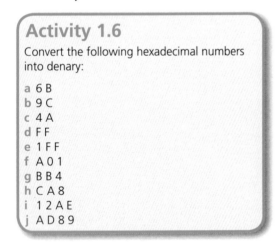

**Activity 1.6**

Convert the following hexadecimal numbers into denary:

a 6 B
b 9 C
c 4 A
d F F
e 1 F F
f A 0 1
g B B 4
h C A 8
i 1 2 A E
j A D 8 9

To convert from denary to hexadecimal is a little more difficult. As with the conversion from binary to denary, there are two very similar methods that can be used. Again, the first method is 'trial and error' and the second method is more methodical and involves repetitive division.

## Method 1

Consider the conversion of the denary number, 2004, into hexadecimal. This method involves placing hexadecimal digits in the appropriate position so that the total equates to 2004:

| 256 | 16 | 1 |
|-----|----|---|
| 7 | D | 4 |

(Note: D = 13)

A quick check shows that: $(7 \times 256) + (13 \times 16) + (4 \times 1)$ gives 2004.

## Method 2

This method involves successive division by 16. The remainders are then read from BOTTOM to TOP to give the hexadecimal value. Again using 2004, we get:

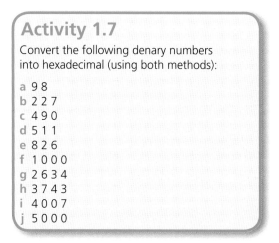

read the remainder from bottom to top to get the hexadecimal number:
7   D   4   (D = 13)

**Figure 1.5**

### Activity 1.7

Convert the following denary numbers into hexadecimal (using both methods):

a 9 8
b 2 2 7
c 4 9 0
d 5 1 1
e 8 2 6
f 1 0 0 0
g 2 6 3 4
h 3 7 4 3
i 4 0 0 7
j 5 0 0 0

## 1.6   Use of the hexadecimal system

This section reviews five uses of the hexadecimal system. The information in this chapter gives the reader sufficient grounding in each topic at this level. Further material can be found by searching the internet, but be careful that you don't go off at a tangent.

## 1.6.1 Memory dumps

Since it is much easier to work with: B 5 A 4 1 A F C

rather than: 1 0 1 1 | 1 0 0 1 | 1 0 1 0 | 0 1 0 0 | 0 0 0 1 | 1 0 1 0 | 1 1 1 1 | 1 1 0 0

hexadecimal is often used when developing new software or when trying to trace errors in programs. The contents of part of the computer memory can hold the key to help solve many problems. When the memory contents are output to a printer or monitor, this is known as a MEMORY DUMP:

| 00990F60 | 54 | 68 | 69 | 73 | 20 | 69 | 73 | 20 | 61 | 6E | 20 | 65 | 78 | 61 | 6D | 70 | 6C | 65 | 20 | 6F | 66 |
|----------|----|----|----|----|----|----|----|----|----|----|----|----|----|----|----|----|----|----|----|----|----|
| 00990F77 | 61 | 20 | 6D | 65 | 6D | 6F | 72 | 79 | 20 | 64 | 75 | 6D | 70 | 20 | 66 | 72 | 6F | 6D | 20 | 20 | 61 |
| 00990E8E | 74 | 79 | 70 | 69 | 63 | 61 | 6C | 20 | 20 | 63 | 6F | 6D | 70 | 75 | 74 | 65 | 72 | 20 | 20 | 6D | 85 |
| 00990EA5 | 6D | 6F | 72 | 79 | 20 | 73 | 68 | 6F | 77 | 69 | 6E | 67 | 20 | 74 | 68 | 65 | 20 | 20 | 63 | 6F | 6E |
| 00990EBC | 74 | 65 | 6E | 74 | 73 | 20 | 6F | 66 | 20 | 61 | 20 | 6E | 75 | 6D | 62 | 65 | 72 | 20 | 20 | 6F | 66 |
| 00990ED3 | 6C | 6F | 63 | 61 | 74 | 69 | 6F | 6E | 73 | 20 | 20 | 69 | 6E | 20 | 20 | 68 | 65 | 78 | 20 | 20 | 20 |
| 00990EEA | 6E | 6F | 74 | 61 | 74 | 69 | 6F | 6E | 20 | 20 | 00 | 00 | 00 | 00 | 00 | 00 | 00 | 00 | 00 | 00 | 00 |

**Figure 1.6**

A program developer can look at each of the hexadecimal codes (as shown in Figure 1.6) and determine where the error lies. The value on the far left shows the memory location so that it is possible to find out exactly where in memory the fault occurs. This is clearly much more manageable using hexadecimal rather than using binary. It's a very powerful fault-tracing tool, but requires considerable knowledge of computer architecture in order to interpret the results.

## 1.6.2 HyperText Mark-up Language (HTML)

HYPERTEXT MARK-UP LANGUAGE (HTML) is used when writing and developing web pages. HTML isn't a programming language but is simply a mark-up language. A mark-up language is used in the processing, definition and presentation of text (for example, specifying the colour of the text).

HTML uses <tags> which are used to bracket a piece of code; for example, <td> starts a standard cell in an HTML table, and </td> ends it. Whatever is between the two tags has been defined. Here is a short section of HTML code:

```
<tr>
    <td><h3>Small car</h3>
        <h3>Used car sales</h3>
        <h2>Cars from $500</h2>
        <br><h2>Cash sales only</h2></td></br>
</tr>
<table border="1">
 <colgroup>
  <col span="2" style="background-color:red">
  <col style="background-color:yellow">
 </colgroup>
```

HTML code is often used to represent colours of text on the computer screen. The values change to represent different colours. The different intensity of the three primary colours (red, green and blue) is determined by its hexadecimal value. For example:

- # FF 00 00 represents primary colour **red**
- # 00 FF 00 represents primary colour green
- # 00 00 FF represents primary colour blue
- # FF 00 FF represents **fuchsia**
- # FF 80 00 represents orange
- # B1 89 04 represents **tan**

and so on producing almost any colour the user wants. There are many websites available that allow a user to find the HTML code for the colour needed.

> ## Activity 1.8
> Using the internet, find the HTML codes for a number of colours.
> Try entering HTML code into the computer and see how the colours and font types can be changed to good effect.
> Make use of websites, such as www.html.am/ to produce your own web pages.
> With a little practice, you can import/embed images into your own design of web page using freely available software.
> Remember this is not a programming language. It is simply a mark-up language, so very little programming skill is required to use HTML.

## 1.6.3 Media Access Control (MAC)

A MEDIA ACCESS CONTROL (**MAC**) ADDRESS refers to a number which uniquely identifies a device on the internet. The MAC address refers to the network interface card (NIC) which is part of the device. The MAC address is rarely changed so that a particular device can always be identified no matter where it is.

A MAC address is usually made up of 48 bits which are shown as six groups of hexadecimal digits (although 64-bit addresses are also known):

NN – NN – NN – DD – DD – DD
or
NN:NN:NN:DD:DD:DD

where the first half (NN – NN – NN) is the identity number of the manufacturer of the device and the second half (DD – DD – DD) is the serial number of the device. For example: 00 – 1C – B3 – 4F – 25 – FE is the MAC address of a device produced by the Apple Corporation (code: 001CB3) with a serial number of 4F25FE. Sometimes lower case hexadecimal letters are used in the MAC address: 00-1c-b3-4f-25-fe. Other manufacturer identity numbers include:

- 00 – 14 – 22 which identifies devices made by Dell
- 00 – 40 – 96 which identifies devices made by Cisco
- 00 – A0 – C9 which identifies devices made by Intel, and so on.

## Types of MAC address

It should be pointed out that there are two types of MAC address: the UNIVERSALLY ADMINISTERED **MAC** ADDRESS (**UAA**) and the LOCALLY ADMINISTERED **MAC** ADDRESS (**LAA**).

The UAA is by far the most common type of MAC address and this is the one set by the manufacturer at the factory. It is rare for a user to want to change this MAC address.

However, there are some occasions when a user or an organisation wishes to change their MAC address. This is a relatively easy task to carry out but it will cause big problems if the changed address isn't unique.

There are a few reasons why the MAC address needs to be changed using LAA:

- Certain software used on mainframe systems needs all the MAC addresses of devices to fall into a strict format; because of this, it may be necessary to change the MAC address of some devices to ensure they follow the correct format.

- It may be necessary to bypass a MAC address filter on a router or a firewall; only MAC addresses with a certain format are allowed through, otherwise the devices will be blocked.
- To get past certain types of network restrictions it may be necessary to emulate unrestricted MAC addresses; hence it may require the MAC address to be changed on certain devices connected to the network.

## 1.6.4 Web addresses

Each character used on a keyboard has what is known as an **ASCII code** (**American Standard Code for Information Interchange**). These codes can be represented using hexadecimal values or decimal values. Figure 1.7 shows part of an ASCII table.

| Dec | Hex | Char | Dec | Hex | Char | Dec | Hex | Char |
|-----|-----|------|-----|-----|------|-----|-----|------|
| 32 | 20 | <SPACE> | 64 | 40 | @ | 96 | 60 | ` |
| 33 | 21 | ! | 65 | 41 | A | 97 | 61 | a |
| 34 | 22 | " | 66 | 42 | B | 98 | 62 | b |
| 35 | 23 | # | 67 | 43 | C | 99 | 63 | c |
| 36 | 24 | $ | 68 | 44 | D | 100 | 64 | d |
| 37 | 25 | % | 69 | 45 | E | 101 | 65 | e |
| 38 | 26 | & | 70 | 46 | F | 102 | 66 | f |
| 39 | 27 | ' | 71 | 47 | G | 103 | 67 | g |
| 40 | 28 | ( | 72 | 48 | H | 104 | 68 | h |
| 41 | 29 | ) | 73 | 49 | I | 105 | 69 | i |
| 42 | 2A | * | 74 | 4A | J | 106 | 6A | j |
| 43 | 2B | + | 75 | 4B | K | 107 | 6B | k |
| 44 | 2C | , | 76 | 4C | L | 108 | 6C | l |
| 45 | 2D | - | 77 | 4D | M | 109 | 6D | m |
| 46 | 2E | . | 78 | 4E | N | 110 | 6E | n |
| 47 | 2F | / | 79 | 4F | O | 111 | 6F | o |
| 48 | 30 | 0 | 80 | 50 | P | 112 | 70 | p |
| 49 | 31 | 1 | 81 | 51 | Q | 113 | 71 | q |
| 50 | 32 | 2 | 82 | 52 | R | 114 | 72 | r |
| 51 | 33 | 3 | 83 | 53 | S | 115 | 73 | s |
| 52 | 34 | 4 | 84 | 54 | T | 116 | 74 | t |
| 53 | 35 | 5 | 85 | 55 | U | 117 | 75 | u |
| 54 | 36 | 6 | 86 | 56 | V | 118 | 76 | v |
| 55 | 37 | 7 | 87 | 57 | W | 119 | 77 | w |
| 56 | 38 | 8 | 88 | 58 | X | 120 | 78 | x |
| 57 | 39 | 9 | 89 | 59 | Y | 121 | 79 | y |
| 58 | 3A | : | 90 | 5A | Z | 122 | 7A | z |
| 59 | 3B | ; | 91 | 5B | [ | 123 | 7B | { |
| 60 | 3C | < | 92 | 5C | \ | 124 | 7C | | |
| 61 | 3D | = | 93 | 5D | ] | 125 | 7D | } |
| 62 | 3E | > | 94 | 5E | ^ | 126 | 7E | ~ |
| 63 | 3F | ? | 95 | 5F | _ | 127 | 7F | <DELETE> |

**Figure 1.7**

A good example of the use of ASCII codes is the representation of a web address (or URL, which stands for uniform resource locator) such as www.hodder.co.uk which becomes (using hexadecimal values):

%77 %77 %77 %2E %68 %6F %64 %64 %65 %72 %2E %63 %6F %2E %75 %6B
 w   w   w   .   h   o   d   d   e   r   .   c   o   .   u   k

(Note: the % sign is used to denote that hexadecimal is being used.)

**Activity 1.9**

Using the ASCII code table (Figure 1.7) convert the following URLs into the equivalent hexadecimal:

a www.cie.org.uk
b www.cie.org.uk/computer_science
c https://www.hodder.co.uk
d www.HodderEducation.co.uk
e http://www.ucles.ac.uk/computing.htm

Sometimes the hexadecimal addresses are used in the address of files or web pages as a security feature. It takes longer to type in the URL using the hexadecimal codes, but it has the advantage that you are unlikely to fall into the trap of copying and pasting a 'fake' website address.

## 1.6.5 Assembly code and machine code

Computer memory can be referred to directly using machine code or assembly code. This can have many advantages to program developers or when carrying out troubleshooting.

Machine code and assembly code are covered in much more detail in Chapter 7; here we are simply interested in how hexadecimal fits into the picture.

Using hexadecimal makes it much easier, faster and less error prone to write code compared to binary. Using true machine code (which uses binary) is very cumbersome and it takes a long time to key in the values. It is also very easy to mistype the digits in a 'sea of 1s and 0s'. Here is a simple example:

STO    FFA4    (assembly code)

A5E4    FFA4    (machine code using hexadecimal values)

1010 0101 1110 0100 1111 1111 1010 0100    (machine code using binary)

Machine code and assembly code are examples of low-level languages and are used by software developers when producing, for example, computer games. As you will find in Chapter 7, although they look cumbersome, they have many advantages at the development stage of software writing (especially when trying to locate errors in the code).

# 2 Communication and internet technologies

In this chapter you will learn about:
- serial and parallel transmission
- error checking after transmission
- web browsers and internet service providers
- http and HTML

## 2.1 Introduction

When data is sent from one device to another, it is important to consider how that data is transmitted. It is also important to ensure that the data hasn't been changed in any way.

The internet has now become an integral part of all of our lives. This chapter will consider some of the important technologies going on in the background which support the internet.

## 2.2 Data transmission

Data transmission can be either over a short distance (for example, from computer to printer) or over longer distances (for example, over a telephone network). Essentially, three factors need to be considered when transmitting data (each factor has to be agreed by both sender and receiver for this to work without error):

- the direction of the data transmission (i.e. in one direction only or in both directions)
- the method of transmission (how many bits are sent at the same time)
- the method of synchronisation between the two devices.

### 2.2.1 Simplex, half-duplex and full-duplex

SIMPLEX DATA TRANSMISSION is in *one direction* only (i.e. from sender to receiver). Example: data being sent from a computer to a printer.

HALF-DUPLEX DATA TRANSMISSION is in *both directions* but *not* at the same time (i.e. data can be sent from 'A' to 'B' or from 'B' to 'A' along the same line, but not at the same time). Example: a phone conversation between two people where only one person speaks at a time.

FULL-DUPLEX DATA TRANSMISSION is in *both directions simultaneously* (i.e. data can be sent from 'A' to 'B' and from 'B' to 'A' along the same line, *both at the same time*). Example: broadband connection on a phone line.

### 2.2.2 Serial and parallel data transmission

SERIAL DATA TRANSMISSION is when data is sent, *one bit at a time*, over *a single wire or channel* (bits are sent one after the other in a single stream).

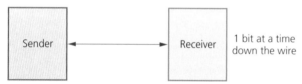

**Figure 2.1**

(Note: bits can be transmitted as simplex, half-duplex or full-duplex.)

This method of data transmission works well over long distances. However, data is transmitted at a slower rate than parallel data transmission. Since only one wire or channel is used, there is no problem of data arriving at its destination out of synchronisation.

An example of its use is sending data from a computer to a modem for transmission over a telephone line.

PARALLEL DATA TRANSMISSION is when *several bits of data (usually 1 byte)* are sent down *several wires or channels at the same time*; one wire or channel is used to transmit each bit.

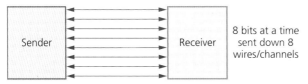

8 bits at a time sent down 8 wires/channels

**Figure 2.2**

**Figure 2.3** Ribbon connector

(Note: bits can be transmitted as simplex, half-duplex or full-duplex.)

This method of data transmission works very well over short distances (over longer distances, the bits can become 'skewed' – this means they will no longer be synchronised). It is, however, a faster method of data transmission than serial.

An example of its use is when sending data to a printer from a computer using a ribbon connector.

---

**Activity 2.1**

Describe what is meant by:

a  serial, half-duplex data transmission
b  parallel, full-duplex data transmission
c  serial, simplex data transmission.

---

A common use for serial data transmission is discussed in Section 2.2.4 (Universal Serial Bus (USB)).

Parallel data transmission is used in the internal electronics of the computer system. The pathways between the CPU and the memory all use this method of data transmission. Integrated circuits, buses and other internal components all use parallel data transmission because of the need for high speed data transfer. The use of 8-bit, 16-bit, 32-bit and 64-bit buses, for example, allow much faster data transmission rates than could be achieved with single channel serial data transfer. An internal clock is used to ensure the correct timing of data transfer; it is essentially synchronous in nature (see Section 2.2.3) and the short distances between components mean that none of the issues described earlier have any real impact on the accuracy of the data.

Chapter 4 covers the internal architecture of computer systems (including the role of buses) and this should be read in conjunction with the information given above.

## 2.2.3 Asynchronous and synchronous data transmission

ASYNCHRONOUS DATA TRANSMISSION refers to data being transmitted in an agreed bit pattern. Data bits (1s and 0s) are grouped together and sent with CONTROL BITS:

| start bit | 1 | 0 | 1 | 1 | 1 | 1 | 0 | 0 | 1 | 1 | 1 | 0 | 1 | 0 | 1 | 0 | stop bit |

control bit                                                                                control bit

**Figure 2.4**

This means that the receiver of the data knows when the data starts and when it ends. This prevents data becoming mixed up; without these control bits, it would be impossible to separate groups of data as they arrived.

SYNCHRONOUS DATA TRANSMISSION is a continuous stream of data (unlike asynchronous data which is sent in discrete groups). The data is accompanied by timing signals generated by an internal clock. This ensures that the sender and receiver are synchronised with each other.

The receiver counts how many bits (1s and 0s) were sent and then reassembles them into bytes of data. The timing must be very accurate here since there are no control bits sent in this type of data transmission. However, it is a faster data transfer method than asynchronous and is therefore used where this is an important issue (for example, in network communications).

## 2.2.4 Universal Serial Bus (USB)

The UNIVERSAL SERIAL BUS (USB) is an asynchronous serial data transmission method. It has quickly become the standard method for transferring data between a computer and a number of devices. Essentially, the USB cable consists of:

- a four-wire shielded cable
- two of the wires are used for power and the earth
- two of the wires are used in the data transmission.

When a device is plugged into a computer using one of the USB ports:

- the computer automatically detects that a device is present (this is due to a small change in the voltage level on the data signal wires in the cable)
- the device is automatically recognised, and the appropriate DEVICE DRIVER is loaded up so that computer and device can communicate effectively
- if a new device is detected, the computer will look for the device driver which matches the device; if this is not available, the user is prompted to download the appropriate software.

**Figure 2.5** USB cable

Even though the USB system has become the industrial standard, there are still a number of benefits (✓) and drawbacks (✗) to using this system:

**Table 2.1**

| ✓ | ✗ |
|---|---|
| Devices plugged into the computer are automatically detected; device drivers are automatically uploaded | – |
| The connectors can only fit one way; this prevents incorrect connections being made | The maximum cable length is presently about 5 metres |
| This has become the industry standard; this means that considerable support is available to users | – |
| Several different data transmission rates are supported | The present transmission rate is limited to less than 500 megabits per second |
| Newer USB standards are backward compatible with older USB standards | The older USB standard (e.g. 1.1) may not be supported in the near future |

## 2.3  Error-checking methods

Following data transmission, there is always the risk that the data has been corrupted or changed in some way. This can occur whether data is being transmitted over short distances or over long distances.

Checking for errors is important since computers aren't able to check that text is correct; they can only recognise whether a word is in their built-in dictionary or not. Look at the following text:

Can you raed tihs?

'I cnduo't bvleiee taht I culod aulaclty uesdtannrd waht I was rdnaieg. Unisg the icndeblire pweor of the hmuan mnid, aocdcrnig to rseecrah at Cmabridge Uinervtisy, it dseno't mttaer in waht oderr the lterets in a wrod are, the olny irpoamtnt tihng is taht the frsit and lsat ltteer be in the rhgit pclae. The rset can be a taotl mses and you can sitll raed it whoutit a pboerlm.

Tihs is bucseae the huamn mnid deos not raed ervey ltteer by istlef, but the wrod as a wlohe.

Aaznmig, huh? Yeah and I awlyas tghhuot slelinpg was ipmorantt! See if yuor fdreins can raed tihs too'

*(From an unknown source at Cambridge University)*

Whilst you probably had little problem understanding this text, a computer would be unable to make any sense of it.

This is why error checking is such an important part of computer technology. This section considers a number of ways that can be used to check for errors so that you don't end up with text as shown in the example above!

A number of methods exist which can detect errors and, in some cases, actually correct the error. The methods covered in this section are:

- parity checking
- automatic repeat request (ARQ)
- checksum
- echo checking.

## 2.3.1 Parity checking

**PARITY CHECKING** is one method used to check whether data has been changed or corrupted following transmission from one device or medium to another device or medium.

A byte of data, for example, is allocated a **PARITY BIT**. This is allocated before transmission takes place. Systems that use **EVEN PARITY** have an even number of 1-bits; systems that use **ODD PARITY** have an odd number of 1-bits. Consider the following byte:

|   | 1 | 1 | 0 | 1 | 1 | 0 | 0 |
|---|---|---|---|---|---|---|---|

parity bit

**Figure 2.6**

If this byte is using even parity, then the parity bit needs to be 0 since there is already an even number of 1-bits (in this case, 4).

If odd parity is being used, then the parity bit needs to be 1 to make the number of 1-bits odd.

Therefore, the byte just before transmission would be:
either (even parity)

| 0 | 1 | 1 | 0 | 1 | 1 | 0 | 0 |
|---|---|---|---|---|---|---|---|

parity bit
**Figure 2.7**

or (odd parity)

| 1 | 1 | 1 | 0 | 1 | 1 | 0 | 0 |
|---|---|---|---|---|---|---|---|

parity bit
**Figure 2.8**

Before data is transferred, an agreement is made between sender and receiver regarding which of the two types of parity are used. This is an example of a PROTOCOL.

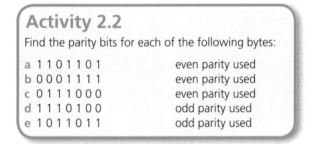

**Activity 2.2**

Find the parity bits for each of the following bytes:

a 1101101       even parity used
b 0001111       even parity used
c 0111000       even parity used
d 1110100       odd parity used
e 1011011       odd parity used

If a byte has been transmitted from 'A' to 'B', and even parity is used, an error would be flagged if the byte now had an odd number of 1-bits at the receiver's end.

## Example 1

sender's byte:

| 0 | 1 | 0 | 1 | 1 | 1 | 0 | 0 |
|---|---|---|---|---|---|---|---|

receiver's byte:

| 0 | 1 | 0 | 0 | 1 | 1 | 0 | 0 |
|---|---|---|---|---|---|---|---|

**Figure 2.9**

In this case, the receiver's byte has three 1-bits, which means it now has odd parity whilst the byte from the sender had even parity (four 1-bits). This clearly means an error has occurred during the transmission of the data.

The error is detected by the computer recalculating the parity of the byte sent. If even parity has been agreed between sender and receiver, then a change of parity in the received byte indicates that a transmission error has occurred.

## Activity 2.3

Which of the following bytes have an error following data transmission?

a  1 1 1 0 1 1 0 1                     even parity used
b  0 1 0 0 1 1 1 1                     even parity used
c  0 0 1 1 1 0 0 0                     even parity used
d  1 1 1 1 0 1 0 0                     odd parity used
e  1 1 0 1 1 0 1 1                     odd parity used

In each case where an error occurs, can you work out which bit is incorrect?

Naturally, *any* of the bits in Example 1 could have been changed leading to a transmission error. Therefore, even though an error has been flagged, it is impossible to know *exactly* which bit is in error. (Your last answer in Activity 2.3 should have been 'NO' since there isn't enough information to determine which bit has been changed.)

 One of the ways around this problem is to use PARITY BLOCKS. In this method, a block of data is sent and the number of 1-bits are totalled horizontally and vertically (in other words, a parity check is done in both horizontal and vertical directions). As Example 2 shows, this method not only identifies that an error has occurred but also indicates where the error is.

# Example 2

In this example, nine bytes of data have been transmitted. Agreement has been made that even parity will be used. Another byte, known as the PARITY BYTE, has also been sent. This byte consists entirely of the parity bits produced by the vertical parity check. The parity byte also indicates the end of the block of data.

The following table shows how the data arrived at the receiving end:

Table 2.2

|            | parity bit | bit 2 | bit 3 | bit 4 | bit 5 | bit 6 | bit 7 | bit 8 |
|------------|------------|-------|-------|-------|-------|-------|-------|-------|
| byte 1     | 1          | 1     | 1     | 1     | 0     | 1     | 1     | 0     |
| byte 2     | 1          | 0     | 0     | 1     | 0     | 1     | 0     | 1     |
| byte 3     | 0          | 1     | 1     | 1     | 1     | 1     | 1     | 0     |
| byte 4     | 1          | 0     | 0     | 0     | 0     | 0     | 1     | 0     |
| byte 5     | 0          | 1     | 1     | 0     | 1     | 0     | 0     | 1     |
| byte 6     | 1          | 0     | 0     | 0     | 1     | 0     | 0     | 0     |
| byte 7     | 1          | 0     | 1     | 0     | 1     | 1     | 1     | 1     |
| byte 8     | 0          | 0     | 0     | 1     | 1     | 0     | 1     | 0     |
| byte 9     | 0          | 0     | 0     | 1     | 0     | 0     | 1     | 0     |
| parity byte | 1         | 1     | 0     | 1     | 0     | 0     | 0     | 1     |

A careful study of Table 2.2 shows the following:

- byte 8 (row 8) has incorrect parity (there are three 1-bits)
- bit 5 (column 5) also has incorrect parity (there are five 1-bits).

First of all, the table shows that an error has occurred following data transmission.

Secondly, at the intersection of row 8 and column 5, the position of the incorrect bit value (which caused the error) can be found.

This means that byte 8 should have the value:

| 0 | 0 | 0 | 1 | **0** | 0 | 1 | 0 |

**Figure 2.10**

which would also correct column 5 giving an even vertical parity (now has four 1-bits).

This byte could therefore be corrected automatically as shown above, or an error message could be relayed back to the sender asking them to retransmit the block of data.

One final point: if two of the bits change value following data transmission, it may be impossible to locate the error using the above method. For example, using Example 1 again:

| 0 | 1 | 0 | 1 | 1 | 1 | 0 | 0 |

**Figure 2.11**

This byte could reach the destination as:

| 0 | 1 | **1** | 1 | 1 | 1 | 0 | **1** |

**Figure 2.12**

or:

| 0 | 1 | 0 | 1 | **0** | **0** | 0 | 0 |

**Figure 2.13**

or:

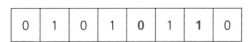

| 0 | 1 | 0 | 1 | **0** | 1 | **1** | 0 |

**Figure 2.14**

All three are clearly incorrect; but they have retained even parity so this wouldn't have triggered an error message at the receiving end. Clearly we need to look at other methods to complement parity when it comes to error checking transmitted data.

## Activity 2.4

The following block of data was received after transmission from a remote computer; odd parity being used by both sender and receiver. One of the bits has been changed during the transmission stage. Locate where this error is and suggest a corrected byte value.

Table 2.3

|  | parity bit | bit 2 | bit 3 | bit 4 | bit 5 | bit 6 | bit 7 | bit 8 |
|---|---|---|---|---|---|---|---|---|
| byte 1 | 0 | 1 | 1 | 0 | 0 | 0 | 1 | 0 |
| byte 2 | 1 | 0 | 1 | 1 | 1 | 1 | 1 | 1 |
| byte 3 | 1 | 0 | 0 | 1 | 1 | 0 | 0 | 0 |
| byte 4 | 0 | 1 | 1 | 0 | 1 | 0 | 1 | 0 |
| byte 5 | 1 | 1 | 1 | 0 | 0 | 1 | 1 | 0 |
| byte 6 | 1 | 0 | 0 | 0 | 0 | 1 | 0 | 1 |
| byte 7 | 0 | 1 | 1 | 1 | 0 | 0 | 0 | 0 |
| byte 8 | 0 | 0 | 0 | 0 | 0 | 0 | 0 | 1 |
| byte 9 | 0 | 1 | 1 | 1 | 1 | 0 | 1 | 0 |
| parity byte | 1 | 0 | 1 | 1 | 1 | 1 | 0 | 0 |

## 2.3.2 Automatic Repeat Request (ARQ)

AUTOMATIC REPEAT REQUEST (ARQ) is another method used to check whether data has been correctly transmitted.

It uses an ACKNOWLEDGEMENT (a message sent by the receiver indicating that data has been received correctly) and TIMEOUT (this is the time allowed to elapse before an acknowledgement is received).

If an acknowledgement isn't sent back to the sender before timeout occurs, then the message is automatically resent.

## 2.3.3 Checksum

CHECKSUM is another way to check if data has been changed or corrupted following data transmission. Data is sent in blocks and an additional value, the checksum, is also sent at the end of the block of data.

To explain how this works, we will assume the checksum of a block of data is 1 byte in length. This gives a maximum value of $2^8 - 1$ (i.e. 255). The value 0000 0000 is ignored in this calculation. Example 3 explains how a checksum is generated.

## Example 3

If the sum of all the bytes in the transmitted block of data is <= 255, then the checksum is this value.

However, if the sum of all the bytes in the data block > 255, then the checksum is found using the simple algorithm in Figure 2.15.

Suppose the value of X is 1185, then tracing through the algorithm, we get:

X = 1185

1 1185/256 = 4.629
2 Rounding down to nearest whole number gives Y = 4
3 Multiplying by 256 gives Z = Y * 256 = 1024
4 The difference (X – Z) gives the checksum: (1185 – 1024) = 161
5 This gives the checksum = 161

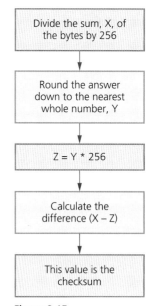

Figure 2.15

When a block of data is about to be transmitted, the checksum for the bytes is first of all calculated. This value is then transmitted with the block of data. At the receiving end, the checksum is recalculated from the block of data received. This calculated value is then compared to the checksum transmitted. If they are the same value, then the data was transmitted without any errors; if the values are different, then a request is sent for the data to be retransmitted.

> **Activity 2.5**
> Calculate the checksum for blocks of data with the following byte sums:
>
> a  148
> b  905
> c  1450
> d  4095

## 2.3.4 Echo check

With ECHO CHECK, when data is sent to another device, this data is sent back again to the sender. The sender compares the two sets of data to check if any errors occurred during the transmission process.

As you will have no doubt worked out, this isn't very reliable. If the two sets of data are different, it isn't known whether the error occurred when sending the data in the first place, or if the error occurred when sending the data back for checking!

However, if no errors occurred then it is another way to check that the data was transmitted correctly.

## 2.4   Internet technologies

The internet is a world-wide system of computer networks and computers. All computers attached to the internet can communicate with each other providing a number of rules and protocols are adhered to.

## 2.4.1 Internet Service Provider (ISP)

Each user makes use of an INTERNET SERVICE PROVIDER (ISP); these are companies that provide the user with access to the internet. A monthly fee is usually charged for this service. The ISP will set up a user account which will contain a username and a password; most ISPs also give the user an email address.

Before ISPs became common in the 1990s, internet access was usually limited to users who were part of a university or a government agency.

# 2.4.2 Internet Protocol (IP) Address

Each device on the internet is given a unique address known as the INTERNET PROTOCOL (IP) ADDRESS. This is a 32-bit number which is usually written in the form:

109.108.158.1

A home computer is given an IP address when it connects to the internet. This is assigned by the ISP and is unique for that particular internet session. The only IP addresses that remain fairly unchanged are web servers.
An IP address can be used instead of typing in the full URL. For example:

http://109.108.158.1

would take you straight to the device corresponding to this address.

## IP addresses and MAC addresses

You will recall the term MEDIA ACCESS CONTROL (MAC) ADDRESS from Chapter 1. This is a unique number that identifies a device connected to the internet. So what is the difference between an IP address and a MAC address? The IP address gives the location of a device on the internet, whereas the MAC address identifies the device connected to the internet.

You can think of the IP address as the address of the house you live in (it will have some unique way of identifying it, such as a post or zip code). Using this example, the MAC address can be thought of as a way of uniquely identifying each person living in that house. It is possible to move house (so your IP address will change) but the same people will be living in the new house (so their MAC addresses will remain unchanged).

# 2.4.3 HTML structure and presentation

When writing HTML code, it is very important to realise that there is a difference between the structure and the presentation.

STRUCTURE is the essential part of the HTML document; it includes the semantics (meaning) and structural mark-up of the document.

PRESENTATION is the style of the document; i.e. how the document will look (or even sound if it includes multimedia elements).

These two features must be kept separate throughout the designing of a web page. At the end of the design process, the author should have an HTML document (which contains the structure and the actual content) and a separate CSS (CASCADING STYLE SHEET) file. The css file will contain everything to control the actual presentation of the web page.

Some of the <tags> used to create a css file have been shown already in the HTML example shown above. The following section shows an example of how these <tags> can be used to create a stylesheet called example2.css. This is then used in a web page document. The tags (h1, h3 and p) all define how the document will look when this css file (stylesheet) is attached.

```
h1      {color:#444400;
                font-family:arial,sans-serif;
                text-align:center;
                font-size:32px}

h3      {color:#000040;
                font-family:serif;
                text-align:justify;
                font-size:16px}

p       {color:#404040;
                font-family:sans-serif;
                text-align:justify;
                font-size:12px}
```

**Figure 2.16** This shows how the css file (example2.css) is created for use in the document below; h1, h3 and p have all been defined, so when the file is attached below, a web browser knows how to display this web page

```
<html>
        <head>
                <link rel="stylesheet" type="text/css" href="example2.css">
        </head>
        <body>
                <td>
                        <h1>This is an example of how to use the html code when setting up a web page.</h1>
                        <h3>The tags are used to define how the document will look.</h3>
                        <p>Paragraphs can be set up using this tag.</p>

                </td>

        </body>
</html>
```

**Figure 2.17**

## 2.4.4 Hypertext transfer protocol (http)

HYPERTEXT TRANSFER PROTOCOL (HTTP) is a set of rules that must be obeyed when transferring files across the internet. When some form of security (e.g. SSL certification or encryption – see Chapter 8) is used, then this changes to https (you also often see the padlock sign 🔒 in the status bar). The letter s after http refers to **http over secure**. It is slower to use https than http; https is usually only adopted where sensitive or private data is being transferred across the internet.

## 2.4.5 Web browsers

A WEB BROWSER is software which allows a user to display a web page on their computer screen. Web browsers interpret or translate the HTML code from websites and show the result of the translation. This can often be in the form of videos, images or sound. Most web browsers share the following features:

- they have a HOME page
- they have the ability to store a user's favourite websites/pages
- they keep a history of the websites visited by the user
- they give the ability to go backward and forward to websites opened.

Users can either click on a link, such as www.hoddereducation.co.uk/igcse or they can type in the uniform resource locator (URL) manually.

The web browser will break up the URL into three parts:

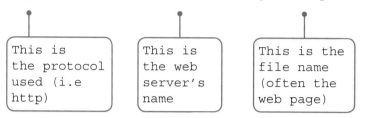

http://www.hoddereducation.co.uk/igcse_computer_science

| This is the protocol used (i.e http) | This is the web server's name | This is the file name (often the web page) |

The web browser translates the web server name into an IP address (see Section 2.4.2) which is part of the URL. The HTML code is returned and is shown as a correctly formatted page on the computer screen. It is also possible that cookies may be sent from the web browser to the web server when the code is executed.

(Note: please refer to Section 8.3 for more information about the use of cookies.)

# 3 Logic gates and logic circuits

In this chapter you will learn about:

- logic gates
- truth tables
- logic circuits
- use of Boolean algebra.

## 3.1 Introduction

Electronic circuits in computers, many new memories and controlling devices are made up of thousands of LOGIC GATES. Logic gates take binary inputs and produce a binary output. Several logic gates combined together form a LOGIC CIRCUIT and these circuits are designed to carry out a specific function.

The checking of the output from a logic gate or logic circuit is done using a TRUTH TABLE.

This chapter will consider the function and role of logic gates, logic circuits and truth tables. Also a number of possible applications of logic circuits will be considered. A reference to BOOLEAN ALGEBRA will be made throughout the chapter, but this is really outside the scope of this textbook. However, Boolean algebra will be seen on many logic gate websites and is included here for completeness.

## 3.2 Logic gates

Six different logic gates will be considered in this chapter:

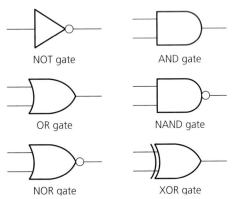

Figure 3.1 Logic gate symbols

## 3.3 Truth tables

Truth tables are used to trace the output from a logic gate or logic circuit. The NOT gate is the only logic gate with one input; the other five gates have two inputs.

When constructing truth tables, all possible combinations of 1s and 0s which can be input are considered. For the NOT gate (one input) there are only $2^1$ (2) possible binary combinations. For all other gates (two inputs), there are $2^2$ (4) possible binary combinations.

For logic circuits, the number of inputs can be more than 2; for example three inputs give a possible $2^3$ (8) binary combinations. And for four inputs, the number of possible binary combinations is $2^4$ (16). It is clear that the number of possible binary combinations is a multiple of the number 2 in every case.

To summarise in table form:

**Table 3.1** Truth tables for two, three and four inputs

| Inputs | |
|---|---|
| A | B |
| 0 | 0 |
| 0 | 1 |
| 1 | 0 |
| 1 | 1 |

| Inputs | | |
|---|---|---|
| A | B | C |
| 0 | 0 | 0 |
| 0 | 0 | 1 |
| 0 | 1 | 0 |
| 0 | 1 | 1 |
| 1 | 0 | 0 |
| 1 | 0 | 1 |
| 1 | 1 | 0 |
| 1 | 1 | 1 |

| Inputs | | | |
|---|---|---|---|
| A | B | C | D |
| 0 | 0 | 0 | 0 |
| 0 | 0 | 0 | 1 |
| 0 | 0 | 1 | 0 |
| 0 | 0 | 1 | 1 |
| 0 | 1 | 0 | 0 |
| 0 | 1 | 0 | 1 |
| 0 | 1 | 1 | 0 |
| 0 | 1 | 1 | 1 |
| 1 | 0 | 0 | 0 |
| 1 | 0 | 0 | 1 |
| 1 | 0 | 1 | 0 |
| 1 | 0 | 1 | 1 |
| 1 | 1 | 0 | 0 |
| 1 | 1 | 0 | 1 |
| 1 | 1 | 1 | 0 |
| 1 | 1 | 1 | 1 |

## 3.4 The function of the six logic gates

### 3.4.1 NOT gate

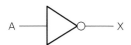

**Figure 3.2**

## Description:

The output, X, is 1 if:

    the input, A, is 0

## Truth table:

**Table 3.2**

| Input | Output |
|---|---|
| A | X |
| 0 | 1 |
| 1 | 0 |

## How to write this:

X = NOT A   (logic notation)

X = $\bar{a}$        (Boolean algebra)

### 3.4.2 AND gate

**Figure 3.3**

## Description:

The output, X, is 1 if:

    both inputs, A and B, are 1

## Truth table:

**Table 3.3**

| Inputs | | Output |
|---|---|---|
| A | B | X |
| 0 | 0 | 0 |
| 0 | 1 | 0 |
| 1 | 0 | 0 |
| 1 | 1 | 1 |

## How to write this:

X = A AND B   (logic notation)

X = a . b      (Boolean algebra)

### 3.4.3 OR gate

**Figure 3.4**

Description:

The output, X, is 1 if:

  either input, A or B, is 1

Truth table:

**Table 3.4**

| Inputs | | Output |
|---|---|---|
| **A** | **B** | **X** |
| 0 | 0 | 0 |
| 0 | 1 | 1 |
| 1 | 0 | 1 |
| 1 | 1 | 1 |

How to write this:

X = A OR B   (logic notation)

X = a + b       (Boolean algebra)

### 3.4.4 NAND gate (NOT AND)

**Figure 3.5**

Description:

The output, X, is 1 if:

  input A AND input B
  are NOT both 1

Truth table:

**Table 3.5**

| Inputs | | Output |
|---|---|---|
| **A** | **B** | **X** |
| 0 | 0 | 1 |
| 0 | 1 | 1 |
| 1 | 0 | 1 |
| 1 | 1 | 0 |

How to write this:

X = A NAND B   (logic notation)

X = $\overline{a \cdot b}$           (Boolean algebra)

### 3.4.5 NOR gate (NOT OR)

**Figure 3.6**

Description:

The output, X, is 1 if:

  neither input A nor
  input B is 1

Truth table:

**Table 3.6**

| Inputs | | Output |
|---|---|---|
| **A** | **B** | **X** |
| 0 | 0 | 1 |
| 0 | 1 | 0 |
| 1 | 0 | 0 |
| 1 | 1 | 0 |

How to write this:

X = A NOR B   (logic notation)

X = $\overline{a + b}$           (Boolean algebra)

# 3.4.6 XOR gate

**Figure 3.7**

## Description:

The output, X, is 1 if:

 (input A is 1 AND input B is 0)
 OR
 (input A is 0 AND input B is 1)

## Truth table:

**Table 3.7**

| Inputs | | Output |
|---|---|---|
| **A** | **B** | **X** |
| 0 | 0 | 0 |
| 0 | 1 | 1 |
| 1 | 0 | 1 |
| 1 | 1 | 0 |

## How to write this:

X = A XOR B (logic notation)

X = (a . $\bar{b}$) + ($\bar{a}$ . b) (Boolean algebra)
(Note: this is sometimes written
as: (a + b) . $\overline{a . b}$)

> ## Activity 3.1
> Find out why X = (a . $\bar{b}$) + ($\bar{a}$ . b) and (a + b) . $\overline{a . b}$ both represent the same logic gate.

(Note: the three symbols in the Boolean algebra have the following meaning:

 .      represents the AND operation
 +      represents the OR operation
 a bar above the letter, e.g. $\bar{a}$, represents the NOT operation.)

# 3.5   Logic circuits

When logic gates are combined together to carry out a particular function, such as controlling a robot, they form a logic circuit.

 The output from the logic circuit is checked using a truth table. There now follows three examples which show:

* how to produce a truth table
* how to design a logic circuit from a given logic statement/Boolean algebra
* how to design a logic circuit to carry out an actual safety function.

# 3.5.1 Example 1

Produce a truth table for the following logic circuit (note the use of . at junctions):

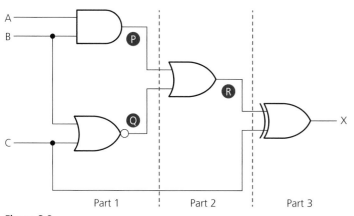

**Figure 3.8**

There are three inputs to this logic circuit, therefore there will be eight possible binary values which can be input.

To show step-wise how the truth table is produced, the logic circuit has been split up into three parts and intermediate values are shown as P, Q and R.

## Part 1

This is the first part of the logic circuit; the first task is to find the intermediate values P and Q.

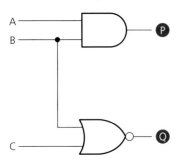

**Figure 3.9**

The value of P is found from the AND gate where the inputs are A and B. The value of Q is found from the NOR gate where the inputs are B and C. An intermediate truth table is produced using the logic function descriptions in Section 3.4.

**Table 3.8**

| Input values | | | Output values | |
|---|---|---|---|---|
| **A** | **B** | **C** | **P** | **Q** |
| 0 | 0 | 0 | 0 | 1 |
| 0 | 0 | 1 | 0 | 0 |
| 0 | 1 | 0 | 0 | 0 |
| 0 | 1 | 1 | 0 | 0 |
| 1 | 0 | 0 | 0 | 1 |
| 1 | 0 | 1 | 0 | 0 |
| 1 | 1 | 0 | 1 | 0 |
| 1 | 1 | 1 | 1 | 0 |

## Part 2

The second part of the logic circuit has P and Q as inputs and the intermediate output, R:

**Figure 3.10**

This produces the following intermediate truth table. (Note: even though there are only two inputs to the logic gate, we have generated eight binary values in part 1 and these must all be used in this second truth table.)

**Table 3.9**

| Inputs | | Output |
|---|---|---|
| **P** | **Q** | **R** |
| 0 | 1 | *1* |
| 0 | 0 | *0* |
| 0 | 0 | *0* |
| 0 | 0 | *0* |
| 0 | 1 | *1* |
| 0 | 0 | *0* |
| 1 | 0 | *1* |
| 1 | 0 | *1* |

# Part 3

The final part of the logic circuit has R and C as inputs and the final output, X:

**Figure 3.11**

This gives the third intermediate truth table:

**Table 3.10**

| Inputs | | Output |
|---|---|---|
| **R** | **C** | **X** |
| 1 | 0 | *1* |
| 0 | 1 | *1* |
| 0 | 0 | *0* |
| 0 | 1 | *1* |
| 1 | 0 | *1* |
| 0 | 1 | *1* |
| 1 | 0 | *1* |
| 1 | 1 | *0* |

Putting all three intermediate truth tables together produces the final truth table which represents the original logic circuit:

**Table 3.11**

| Input values | | | Intermediate values | | | Output |
|---|---|---|---|---|---|---|
| **A** | **B** | **C** | **P** | **Q** | **R** | **X** |
| 0 | 0 | 0 | *0* | *1* | *1* | 1 |
| 0 | 0 | 1 | *0* | *0* | *0* | 1 |
| 0 | 1 | 0 | *0* | *0* | *0* | 0 |
| 0 | 1 | 1 | *0* | *0* | *0* | 1 |
| 1 | 0 | 0 | *0* | *1* | *1* | 1 |
| 1 | 0 | 1 | *0* | *0* | *0* | 1 |
| 1 | 1 | 0 | *1* | *0* | *1* | 1 |
| 1 | 1 | 1 | *1* | *0* | *1* | 0 |

The intermediate values can be left out of the final truth table, but it is good practice to leave them in until you become confident about producing the truth tables. The final truth table would then look like this:

**Table 3.12**

| Input values | | | Output |
|---|---|---|---|
| A | B | C | X |
| 0 | 0 | 0 | 1 |
| 0 | 0 | 1 | 1 |
| 0 | 1 | 0 | 0 |
| 0 | 1 | 1 | 1 |
| 1 | 0 | 0 | 1 |
| 1 | 0 | 1 | 1 |
| 1 | 1 | 0 | 1 |
| 1 | 1 | 1 | 0 |

## Activity 3.2

Produce truth tables for each of the following logic circuits. You are advised to split them up into intermediate parts to help eliminate errors.

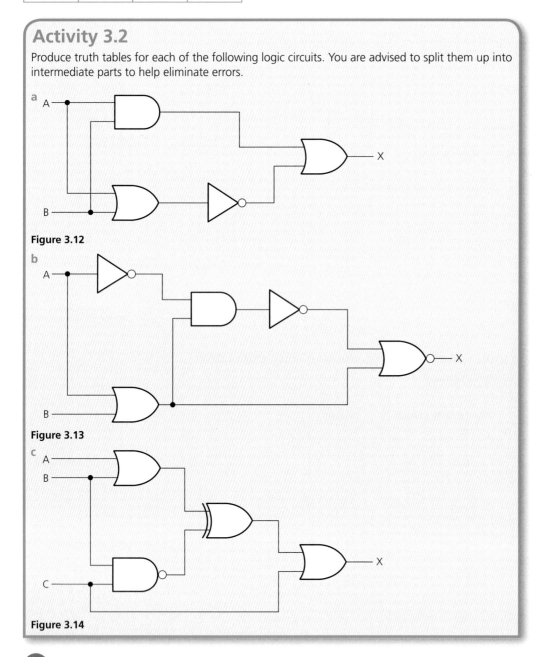

a

**Figure 3.12**

b

**Figure 3.13**

c

**Figure 3.14**

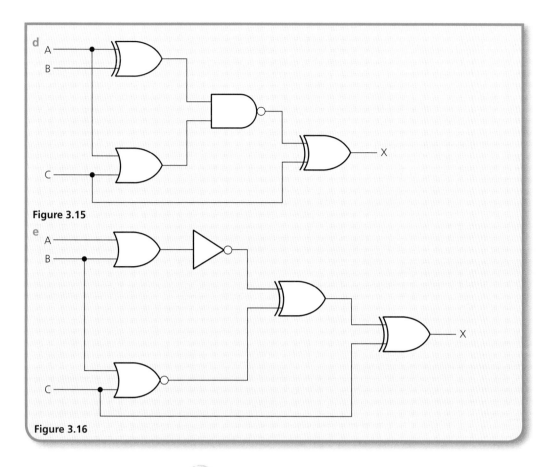

**Figure 3.15**

**Figure 3.16**

## 3.5.2 Example 2 ⦾

A safety system uses three inputs to a logic circuit. An alarm, X, sounds if input A represents ON and input B represents OFF; or if input B represents ON and input C represents OFF.

Produce a logic circuit and truth table to show the conditions which cause the output X to be 1.

The first thing to do is to write down the logic statement representing the scenario in this example. To do this, it is necessary to recall that ON = 1 and OFF = 0 and also that 0 is usually considered to be NOT 1.

So we get the following logic statement:

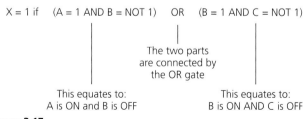

X = 1 if    (A = 1 AND B = NOT 1)    OR    (B = 1 AND C = NOT 1)

The two parts
are connected by
the OR gate

This equates to:                    This equates to:
A is ON and B is OFF          B is ON AND C is OFF

**Figure 3.17**

Note: this statement can also be written in Boolean algebra as:

$$(a \cdot \bar{b}) + (b \cdot \bar{c})$$

The logic circuit is made up of three parts as shown in the logic statement. We will produce the logic gate for the first part and the third part. Then join both parts together with the OR gate.

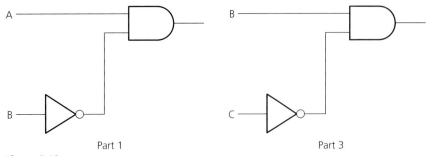

**Figure 3.18**

Now combining both parts with the OR gate gives us:

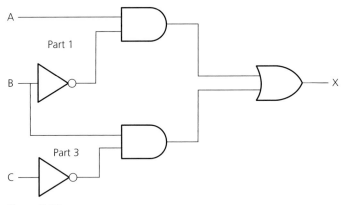

**Figure 3.19**

There are two ways to produce the truth table:

- trace through the logic circuit using the method described in Example 1 (Section 3.5.1)
- produce the truth table using the original logic statement; this second method has the advantage that it allows you to check that your logic circuit is correct.

We will use the second method in this example:

**Table 3.13**

| Inputs | | | Intermediate values | | Output |
|---|---|---|---|---|---|
| A | B | C | (A=1 AND B=NOT 1) | (B=1 AND C=NOT 1) | X |
| 0 | 0 | 0 | 0 | 0 | 0 |
| 0 | 0 | 1 | 0 | 0 | 0 |
| 0 | 1 | 0 | 0 | 1 | 1 |
| 0 | 1 | 1 | 0 | 0 | 0 |
| 1 | 0 | 0 | 1 | 0 | 1 |
| 1 | 0 | 1 | 1 | 0 | 1 |
| 1 | 1 | 0 | 0 | 1 | 1 |
| 1 | 1 | 1 | 0 | 0 | 0 |

(Note: it is optional to leave in the intermediate values or to remove them giving a four-column truth table with headings: A, B, C, X.)

> ## Activity 3.3
> Draw the logic circuits and complete the truth tables for the following logic statements and Boolean algebra statements:
>
> a X = 1 if (A = 1 OR B = 1) OR (A = 0 AND B = 1)
> b Y = 1 if (A = 0 AND B = 0) AND (B = 0 OR C = 1)
> c T = 1 if (switch K is ON or switch L is ON) OR (switch K is ON and switch M is OFF) OR (switch M is ON)
> d $x = (a \cdot \overline{b}) + (\overline{b} \cdot c)$
> e R = 1 if (switch A is ON and switch B is ON) AND (switch B is ON or switch C is OFF)

## 3.5.3 Example 3

A wind turbine has a safety system which uses three inputs to a logic circuit. A certain combination of conditions results in an output, X, from the logic circuit being equal to 1. When the value of X = 1 then the wind turbine is shut down.

The following table shows which parameters are being monitored and form the three inputs to the logic circuit.

**Table 3.14**

| Parameter description | Parameter | Binary value | Description of condition |
|---|---|---|---|
| turbine speed | S | 0 | <= 1000 rpm |
|  |  | 1 | > 1000 rpm |
| bearing temperature | T | 0 | <= 80°C |
|  |  | 1 | > 80°C |
| wind velocity | W | 0 | <= 120 kph |
|  |  | 1 | > 120 kph |

The output, X, will have a value of 1 if any of the following combination of conditions occur:

- **either** turbine speed <= 1000 rpm and bearing temperature > 80°C
- **or** turbine speed > 1000 rpm and wind velocity > 120 kph
- **or** bearing temperature <= 80°C and wind velocity > 120 kph.

Design the logic circuit and complete the truth table to produce a value of X =1 when any of the three conditions above occur.

This is a different type of problem to those covered in Examples 1 and 2. This time a real situation is given and it is necessary to convert the information into a logic statement and then produce the logic circuit and truth table. It is advisable in problems as complex as this to produce the logic circuit and truth table separately (based on the conditions given) and then check them against each other to see if there are any errors.

## Stage 1

The first thing to do is to convert each of the three statements into logic statements. Use the information given in the table and the three condition statements to find how the three parameters, S, T and W, are linked. We usually look for the key words AND, OR and NOT when converting actual statements into logic.

We end up with the following three logic statements:

i turbine speed <= 1000 rpm and bearing temperature > 80°C
   logic statement: (S = NOT 1 AND T = 1)
ii turbine speed > 1000 rpm and wind velocity > 120 kph
   logic statement: (S = 1 AND W = 1)
iii bearing temperature <= 80°C and wind velocity > 120 kph
   logic statement: (T = NOT 1 AND W = 1)

## Stage 2

This now produces three intermediate logic circuits:

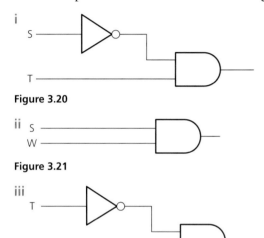

**Figure 3.20**

**Figure 3.21**

**Figure 3.22**

Each of the three original statements were joined together by the word OR. Thus we need to join all of the three intermediate logic circuits by two OR gates to get the final logic circuit.

We will start by joining (i) and (ii) together using an OR gate:

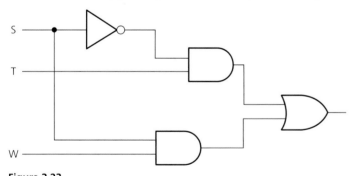

**Figure 3.23**

Finally, we connect the logic circuit in Figure 3.23 to Figure 3.22 to obtain the answer:

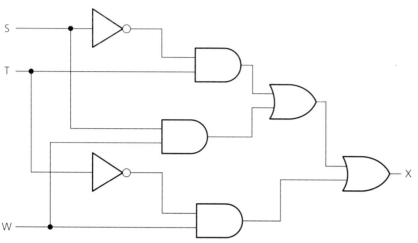

**Figure 3.24**

The final part is to produce the truth table. We will do this using the original logic statement. This method has the bonus of allowing an extra check to be made on the logic circuit in Figure 3.24 to see whether or not it is correct. It is possible, however, to produce the truth table straight from the logic circuit in Figure 3.24.

There were three parts to the problem, so the truth table will first evaluate each part. Then, by applying OR gates, as shown below, the final value, X, is obtained:

i  (S = NOT 1 AND T = 1)
ii  (S = 1 AND W = 1)
iii (T = NOT 1 AND W = 1)

We find the outputs from parts (i) and (ii) and then OR these two outputs together to obtain a new intermediate, which we will label part (iv).

We then OR parts (iii) and (iv) together to get the value of X.

**Table 3.15**

| Inputs | | | Intermediate values | | | | Output |
|---|---|---|---|---|---|---|---|
| S | T | W | (i) (S=NOT 1 AND T=1) | (ii) (S=1 AND W=1) | (iii) (T=NOT 1 AND W=1) | (iv) | X |
| 0 | 0 | 0 | 0 | 0 | 0 | 0 | 0 |
| 0 | 0 | 1 | 0 | 0 | 1 | 0 | 1 |
| 0 | 1 | 0 | 1 | 0 | 0 | 1 | 1 |
| 0 | 1 | 1 | 1 | 0 | 0 | 1 | 1 |
| 1 | 0 | 0 | 0 | 0 | 0 | 0 | 0 |
| 1 | 0 | 1 | 0 | 1 | 1 | 1 | 1 |
| 1 | 1 | 0 | 0 | 0 | 0 | 0 | 0 |
| 1 | 1 | 1 | 0 | 1 | 0 | 1 | 1 |

## Activity 3.4

Two scenarios are described below. In each case, produce the logic circuit and complete a truth table to represent the scenario.

a A chemical process is protected by a logic circuit. There are three inputs to the logic circuit representing key parameters in the chemical process. An alarm, X, will give an output value of 1 depending on certain conditions in the chemical process. The following table describes the process conditions being monitored:

**Table 3.16**

| Parameter description | Parameter | Binary value | Description of condition |
|---|---|---|---|
| chemical reaction rate | R | 0 | reaction rate < 40 mol/l/sec |
| | | 1 | reaction rate >= 40 mol/l/sec |
| process temperature | T | 0 | temperature > 115°C |
| | | 1 | temperature <= 115°C |
| concentration of chemicals | C | 0 | concentration = 4 mol |
| | | 1 | concentration > 4 mol |

An alarm, X, will generate the value 1 if:
either
reaction rate < 40 mol/l/sec
or
concentration > 4 mol AND temperature > 115°C
or
reaction rate >= 40 mol/l/sec AND temperature > 115°C

b A power station has a safety system controlled by a logic circuit. Three inputs to the logic circuit determine whether the output, S, is 1. When S = 1 the power station shuts down. The following table describes the conditions being monitored.

**Table 3.17**

| Parameter description | Parameter | Binary value | Description of condition |
|---|---|---|---|
| gas temperature | G | 0 | gas temperature <= 160°C |
| | | 1 | gas temperature > 160°C |
| reactor pressure | R | 0 | reactor pressure <= 10 bar |
| | | 1 | reactor pressure > 10 bar |
| water temperature | W | 0 | water temperature <= 120°C |
| | | 1 | water temperature > 120°C |

Output, S, will generate a value of 1, if:
either
gas temperature > 160°C AND water temperature <= 120°C
or
gas temperature <= 160°C AND reactor pressure > 10 bar
or
water temperature > 120°C AND reactor pressure > 10 bar

## 3.6   Logic circuits in the real world

Anybody with an electronics background who is reading this chapter will be aware that the design of logic circuits is considerably more complex than has been described.

This chapter has described in detail some of the fundamental theories used in logic circuit design. This will give the reader sufficient grounding to cover all existing (I)GCSE and O level syllabuses. However, it is worth finally discussing some of the more advanced aspects of logic circuit design.

Electronics companies need to consider the cost of components, ease of fabrication and time constraints when designing and building logic circuits.

We will mention two possible ways electronics companies can review logic circuit design:

1 One method is to use 'off-the-shelf' logic units and build up the logic circuit as a number of 'building blocks'.
2 Another method involves simplifying the logic circuit as far as possible; this may be necessary where room is at a premium (e.g. in building circuit boards for use in satellites to allow space exploration).

## 3.6.1 Using logic 'building blocks'

One very common 'building block' is the NAND gate. It is possible to build up any logic gate, and therefore any logic circuit, by simply linking together a number of NAND gates. For example, the AND, OR and NOT gates can be built from these gates as shown below:

The AND gate:

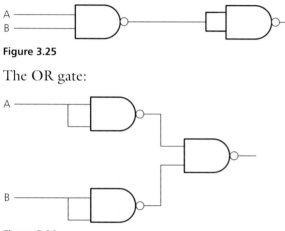

**Figure 3.25**

The OR gate:

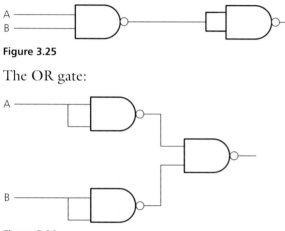

**Figure 3.26**

The NOT gate:

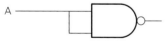

**Figure 3.27**

## Activity 3.5

By drawing the truth tables, show that the three circuits above can be used to represent AND, OR and NOT gates.

## Activity 3.6

a  Show how the following logic circuit could be built using NAND gates only.
Also complete truth tables for both logic circuits to show that they produce identical outputs.

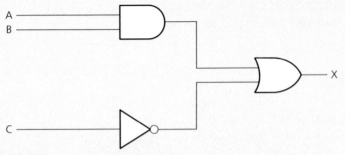

**Figure 3.28**

b  Show how the XOR gate could be built from NAND gates only.
c  Complete a truth table for your final design to show it that it produces the same output as a
single XOR gate.

## Activity 3.7

Show by drawing a truth table which single logic gate has the same function as the following
logic circuit made up of NAND gates only.

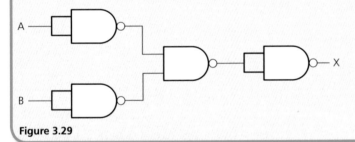

**Figure 3.29**

# 3.6.2 Simplification of logic circuits

The second method involves the simplification of logic circuits. By reducing the
number of components, the cost of production can be less. This can also improve
reliability and make it easier to trace faults if they occur.

The following example (Figure 3.30) can be simplified to a single gate. You are
asked to show how this can be done in Activity 3.8.

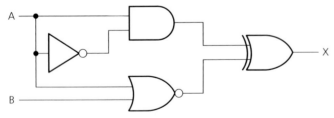

**Figure 3.30**

## Activity 3.8

Show by drawing a truth table which single logic gate has the same function as the logic circuit drawn in Figure 3.30.

## Activity 3.9

Complete the truth table for the following logic circuit and then consider what simplified design could replace the whole logic circuit.

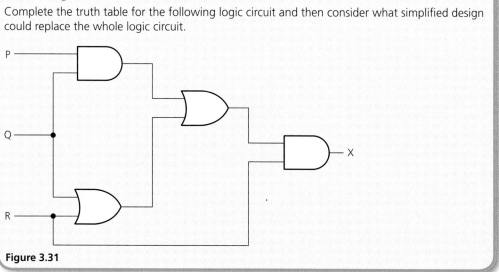

**Figure 3.31**

# 4 Operating systems and computer architecture

In this chapter you will learn about:

● operating systems
● interrupts and buffers
● computer architecture and the von Neumann computer model
● the fetch–execute cycle.

## 4.1 Introduction

All modern computers have some form of operating system which users generally take for granted. The operating system makes it possible to communicate with the software and hardware that make up a typical computer system.

There are many ways of representing computer architecture, but one of the more common ones is known as the von Neumann model which will be fully described in this chapter.

## 4.2 Operating systems

The **OPERATING SYSTEM (OS)** is essentially software running in the background of a computer system. It manages many of the basic functions which are shown in Figure 4.1. Obviously not all operating systems carry out everything shown in the figure but it gives some idea of the importance and complexity of this software. Without it, most computers would be very user-unfriendly and the majority of users would find it almost impossible to work with computers on a day-to-day basis.

**Figure 4.1**

One of the most common examples of an operating system is known as Windows and is used on many personal computers. Other examples include: Linux, Android, UNIX and DOS. Windows is an example of a single-user multitasking operating system – this means only one user can use the computer at a time but can have many applications open simultaneously. How operating systems actually work is beyond the scope of this textbook.

When a computer is first powered up, the initiating programs are loaded into memory from the ROM (read only memory) chip. These programs run a checking procedure to make sure the hardware, processor, internal memory and bios (basic input–output system) are all functioning correctly. If no errors are detected, then the operating system is loaded into memory.

It is worth mentioning here that simple devices with embedded microprocessors don't always have an operating system. Household items, such as cookers, microwave ovens and washing machines only carry out single tasks which don't vary. The input is usually a button pressed or a touchscreen option selected which activates a simple hardware function which doesn't need an operating system to control it.

> ## Activity 4.1
> Find out how appliances fitted with microprocessors can be controlled and activated by web-enabled devices such as smart phones.

## 4.3  Interrupts and buffers

An INTERRUPT is a signal sent from a device or from software to the processor. This will cause the processor to temporarily stop what it is doing and service the interrupt. Interrupts can occur when, for example:

- a disk drive is ready to receive more data
- an error has occurred, such as a paper jam in a printer
- the user has pressed a key to interrupt the current process – an example could be <CTRL><ALT><BREAK> keys pressed simultaneously
- a software error has occurred – an example of this would be if an .exe file couldn't be found to initiate the execution of a program.

Once the interrupt signal is received, the processor either carries on with what it was doing or stops to service the device/program that generated the interrupt.

Interrupts allow computers to carry out many tasks or to have several windows open at the same time. An example would be downloading a file from the internet at the same time as listening to some music from the computer library. Whenever an interrupt is serviced, the status of the current task being run is saved. This is done using an INTERRUPT HANDLER and once the interrupt has been fully serviced, the status of the interrupted task is reinstated and it continues from the point prior to the interrupt being sent.

BUFFERS are used in computers as a temporary memory area. These are essential in modern computers since hardware devices operate at much slower speeds than the processor. If it wasn't for buffers, processors would spend the majority of their time idle, waiting for the hardware device to complete its operation. Buffers are essentially filled from the processor or memory unit and whilst these are emptied to the hardware device, the processor carries on with other tasks. Buffers are used, for example, when streaming a video from the internet. This ensures that the video playback doesn't keep on stopping to wait for data from the internet.

Buffers and interrupts are often used together to allow standard computer functions to be carried out. These functions are often taken for granted by users of modern computer systems. Figure 4.2 shows how buffers and interrupts are used when a document is sent to a printer.

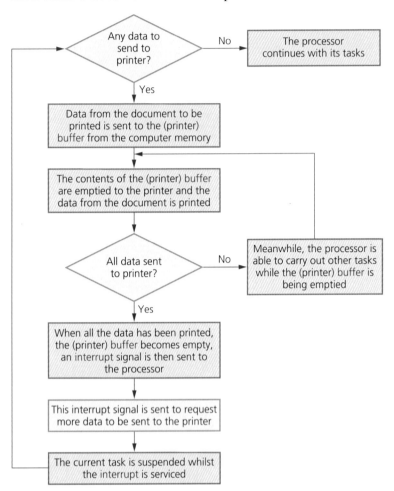

**Figure 4.2**

## Activity 4.2

Find out how buffers and interrupts are used when sending data to memories such as DVDs and solid state (e.g. pen drive).

## Activity 4.3

Find out how buffers are used when streaming a video or music from the internet to your computer.

## Activity 4.4

Investigate the many ways that hardware and software can cause an interrupt to occur. Are ALL interrupts treated equally or do some have priority over others?

## 4.4 Computer architecture

Very early computers were fed data whilst the machines were actually running. They weren't able to store programs; consequently, they weren't able to run without human intervention. In about 1945, John von Neumann developed the idea of a stored program computer, often referred to as the VON NEUMANN ARCHITECTURE concept. His idea was to hold programs and data in a memory. Data would then move between the memory unit and the processor.

There are many diagrams which show von Neumann architecture. Figures 4.3 and 4.4 show two different ways of representing this computer model. The first diagram is a fairly simple model whereas the second diagram goes into more detail.

Figure 4.3 shows the idea of how a processor and memory unit are linked together by connections known as BUSES. This is a simple representation of von Neumann architecture. These connections are described in Table 4.1.

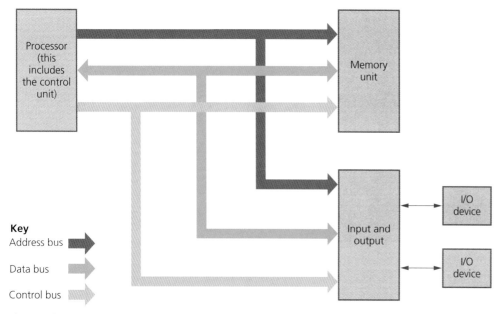

**Figure 4.3**

Table 4.1 describes the function of each of the three buses shown in Figure 4.3. Buses essentially move data around the computer and also send out control signals to make sure everything is properly synchronised.

**Table 4.1**

| Type of bus | Description of bus | Data/signal direction |
|---|---|---|
| address bus | carries signals relating to addresses (see later) between the processor and the memory | unidirectional (signals travel in one direction only) |
| data bus | sends data between the processor, the memory unit and the input/ output devices | bi-directional (data can travel in both directions) |
| control bus | carries signals relating to the control and coordination of all activities within the computer (examples include: the read and write functions) | this is regarded as being both unidirectional and bi-directional due to the internal connections within the computer architecture |

Figure 4.4 shows a slightly more detailed diagram of the von Neumann architecture. It brings to our attention another new concept in this computer model – the idea of ADDRESSES and REGISTERS. Addresses indicate where the data is stored and registers are needed so that data can be manipulated within the computer.

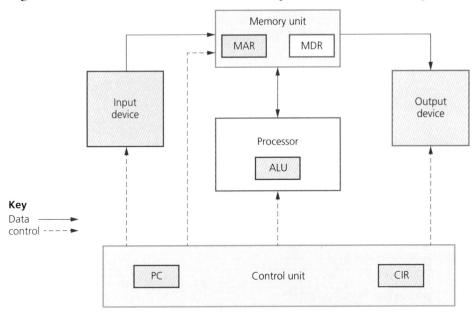

Please note: registers are shown in the diagram as a form of representation and don't actually reflect computer architecture. This is a simplification to help understand the following chapter notes.

**Figure 4.4**

An address is the location of where data can be found in a computer memory. Each address in the memory is unique. The addresses aren't actually shown in Figure 4.4, but they are contained in the part of the diagram labelled memory unit. The actual function of the addresses is discussed in Section 4.4.1.

You will notice a number of items shown in the diagram known as registers: MAR, MDR, ALU, PC and CIR. These are a little more complex and their function will be fully described in the following pages. But essentially a register is simply a high-speed storage area within the computer. All data must be represented in a register before it can be processed. For example, if two numbers are to be added, both numbers must be stored in registers and the result of the addition must also be stored in a register.

## Activity 4.5

Draw up a summary table that shows how buses, registers and addresses are all connected together. This can be done by doing a desk-top exercise:

- Use a sheet of A0 (flipchart size) paper and draw a large outline of the FIVE main components shown in Figure 4.4.
- Cut coloured arrows out of cardboard to show the buses and place on the diagram you've just drawn; the data and control buses will be easy to fit.
- However, you will need to do a little bit of thinking to decide how the address bus fits into your diagram.
- Cut the five registers out of cardboard and place them on the large A0 outline.
- Above the memory unit, place an example of some memory addresses and their contents.
- Cut out some 8-bit binary numbers representing your addresses and contents.
- Finally by moving data around you should be able to see how buses, addresses and registers all interconnect; you get further help in doing this desk-top exercise when you read Sections 4.4.1 to 4.4.4.
- Try to find out how simple operations like addition can be carried out using your desk-top exercise.

## 4.4.1 Memory unit

The computer memory unit is made up of a number of partitions. Each partition consists of an ADDRESS and its CONTENTS. The example shown here uses 8 bits for each address and 8 bits for the content. In a real computer memory, the address and its contents are actually much larger than this.

The address will uniquely identify every LOCATION in the memory and the contents will be the binary value stored in each location.

**Table 4.2**

| Address | Contents |
|---|---|
| 1111 0000 | 0111 0010 |
| 1111 0001 | 0101 1011 |
| 1111 0010 | 1101 1101 |
| 1111 0011 | 0111 1011 |
| ↓ | ↓ |
| 1111 1100 | 1110 1010 |
| 1111 1101 | 1001 0101 |
| 1111 1110 | 1000 0010 |
| 1111 1111 | 0101 0101 |

Figure 4.4 showed five examples of registers. Their function will be described later on, but for now, the abbreviations stand for:

- MAR memory address register
- MDR memory data register
- ALU arithmetic and logic unit
- PC program counter
- CIR current instruction register.

Let us now consider how the two registers (MAR and MDR) shown in the memory unit are used.

Consider the READ operation. We will use the memory section shown in Table 4.2. Suppose we want to read the contents of memory location 1111 0001; the two registers are used as follows:

- The address of location 1111 0001 to be read from is first written into the MAR (memory address register):

**Figure 4.5**

- A 'read signal' is sent to the computer memory using the control bus.
- The contents of memory location 1111 0001 are then put into the MDR (memory data register):

(Look at Table 4.2 to confirm this.)

**Figure 4.6**

Now let us consider the WRITE operation. Again we will use the memory section shown in Table 4.2. Suppose this time we want to show how the value 1001 0101 was written into memory location 1111 1101.

- The data to be stored is first written into the MDR (memory data register):

MDR: | 1 | 0 | 0 | 1 | 0 | 1 | 0 | 1 |

**Figure 4.7**

- This data has to be written into the memory location with the address 1111 1101; so this address is now written into the MAR:

MAR: | 1 | 1 | 1 | 1 | 1 | 1 | 0 | 1 |

**Figure 4.8**

- Finally, a 'write signal' is sent to the computer memory using the control bus and this value will then be written into the correct memory location. (Again confirm this by looking at Table 4.2.)

> ## Activity 4.6
> Use your model created in Activity 4.5 to show how the two operations, read and write, are carried out in the von Neumann architecture.

## 4.4.2 Processor

The PROCESSOR contains the ARITHMETIC AND LOGIC UNIT (ALU). The ALU allows arithmetic (e.g. add, subtract, etc.) and logic (e.g. AND, OR, NOT, etc.) operations to be carried out. How this is used is explained in Section 4.5.

## 4.4.3 Control unit

The CONTROL UNIT controls the operation of the memory, processor and input/output devices.

Essentially, the control unit reads an instruction from memory (the address of the location where the instruction can be found is stored in the Program Counter (PC)). This instruction is then interpreted. During that process, signals are generated along the control bus to tell the other components in the computer what to do.

How this all fits together with the other components of the von Neumann model is discussed in Section 4.5.

## 4.4.4 Input and output devices

The input and output devices are discussed in Chapter 5 and are the main method of entering data into and getting data out of computer systems. Input devices convert external data into a form the computer can understand and can then process (e.g. keyboards, touchscreens and microphones). Output devices show the results of computer processing in a humanly understandable form (e.g. printers, monitors and loudspeakers).

How all of these five registers are used by a typical computer system can be found in Section 4.5 – the fetch–execute cycle. Again other textbooks and websites will all have different ways of showing how this cycle operates. The important thing is to get a good general understanding of how the cycle functions.

# 4.5 The fetch–execute cycle

To carry out a set of instructions, the processor first of all FETCHES some data and instructions from memory and stores them in suitable registers. Both the address bus and the data bus are used in this process. Once this is done, each instruction needs to be decoded before finally being EXECUTED. This is all known as the FETCH–EXECUTE CYCLE and is the last part of this puzzle.

The CURRENT INSTRUCTION REGISTER (CIR) contains the *current* instruction being proceed. THE PROGRAM COUNTER (PC) contains the address of the *next* instruction to be executed.

## Fetch

In the fetch–execute cycle, the next instruction is fetched from the memory address currently stored in the Program Counter (PC) and is then stored in the Current Instruction Register (CIR). The PC is then incremented (increased by 1) so that the next instruction can be processed.

This is then decoded so that each instruction can be interpreted in the next part of the cycle.

## Execute

The processor passes the decoded instruction as a set of control signals to the appropriate components within the computer system. This allows each instruction to be carried out in its logical sequence.

Figure 4.9 shows how the fetch–execute cycle is carried out in the von Neumann computer model. As with most aspects of computer science, there will be slight variations on this diagram if other textbooks or websites are consulted. The main aim is to end up with a clear understanding of how this cycle works.

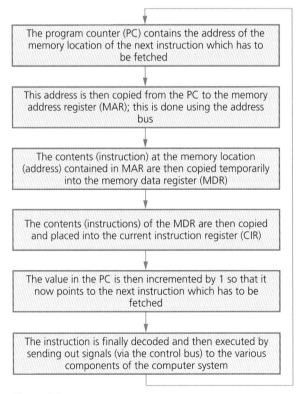

**Figure 4.9**

Figure 4.9 shows the actual stages that take place during the fetch–execute cycle, showing how each of the registers and buses are used in the process (the first five boxes are part of the fetch cycle and the last box is part of the execute cycle).

## Activity 4.7

- It is worth trying to do a desk-top exercise to carry out a series of instructions using the fetch–execute cycle. Do some research and decide on four or five operations (add, subtract, etc.) and give the 8-bit binary codes. Then create a memory map as shown in Activity 4.5.
- Once this is done, use the five registers you created in Activity 4.5 and new 8-bit binary values to trace out exactly what happens as instructions are fetched and executed in your computer model.

# 5  Input and output devices

In this chapter you will learn about:

- input devices
- applications of input devices
- output devices
- applications of output devices.

## 5.1  Introduction

Computer systems would be of little real use without a method of input or output. This chapter reviews how a number of input and output devices work. It also considers a variety of applications which make use of these devices.

The input devices covered include:

- scanners
- barcode readers/scanners
- quick response (QR) code readers
- digital cameras
- keyboards
- pointing devices (such as a mouse)
- microphones
- touchscreens
- sensors
- interactive whiteboards.

The output devices covered include:

- inkjet printers
- laser printers
- 3D printers
- 2D/3D cutters
- actuators
- loudspeakers
- LCD/LED monitors
- projectors (LCD and DLP).

## 5.2  Input devices

### 5.2.1 Scanners

SCANNERS are either two-dimensional (2D) or three-dimensional (3D).

#### Two-dimensional scanners

These types of scanner are the most common form and are generally used to input hard-copy (paper) documents. The image is converted into an electronic form which can be stored in a computer.

A number of stages occur when scanning a document:

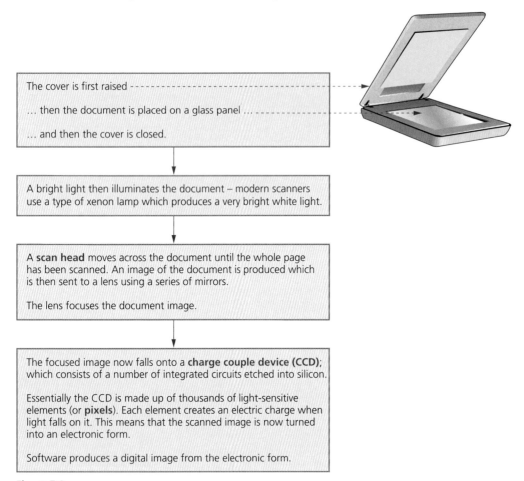

The cover is first raised - - - - - - - - - - - - - - - - - - - - - - - - - - - - - - - - - - - - - - - →

... then the document is placed on a glass panel ... - - - - - - - - - - - - - →

... and then the cover is closed.

A bright light then illuminates the document – modern scanners use a type of xenon lamp which produces a very bright white light.

A **scan head** moves across the document until the whole page has been scanned. An image of the document is produced which is then sent to a lens using a series of mirrors.

The lens focuses the document image.

The focused image now falls onto a **charge couple device (CCD)**; which consists of a number of integrated circuits etched into silicon.

Essentially the CCD is made up of thousands of light-sensitive elements (or **pixels**). Each element creates an electric charge when light falls on it. This means that the scanned image is now turned into an electronic form.

Software produces a digital image from the electronic form.

**Figure 5.1**

Computers equipped with OPTICAL CHARACTER RECOGNITION (**OCR**) software allow the scanned text from the document to be converted into a TEXT FILE FORMAT. This means the scanned image can now be edited and manipulated by importing it into a word processor.

If the original document was a photograph or image, then the scanned image forms an image file such as JPEG (see Section 6.2.3).

## Three-dimensional scanners

3D scanners scan solid objects and produce a three-dimensional image. Since solid objects have $x$, $y$ and $z$ coordinates, these scanners take images at several points along these three coordinates. A digital image which represents the solid object is formed.

The scanned images can be used in COMPUTER AIDED DESIGN (**CAD**) or, more recently, sent to a 3D printer (see Section 5.3.3) to produce a working model of the scanned image.

There are numerous technologies used in 3D scanners – lasers, magnetic resonance, white light, and so on. It is beyond the scope of this book to look at these in any great depth; however, the second application that follows describes the technology behind one form of 3D scanning.

# Application of 2D scanners at an airport

2D scanners are used at airports to read passports. They make use of OCR technology to produce digital images which represent the passport pages. Because of the OCR technology, these digital images can be manipulated in a number of ways.

For example, the OCR software is able to review these images, select the text part and then automatically put the text into the correct fields of an existing database. It is possible for the text to be stored in ASCII format (see Chapter 1) – it all depends on how the data is to be used.

At many airports the two-dimensional photograph in the passport is also scanned and stored as a jpeg image. The passenger's face is also photographed using a digital camera (a 2D image is taken so it can be matched to the image taken from the passport). The two digital images are compared using face recognition/detection software. Key parts of the face are compared.

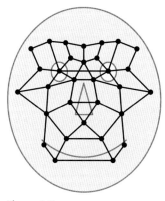

**Figure 5.2**

The face in Figure 5.2 shows several of the positions used by the face recognition software. Each position is checked when the software tries to compare two facial images. Data such as:

- distance between the eyes
- width of the nose
- shape of the cheek bones
- length of the jaw line
- shape of the eyebrows

are all used to identify a given face.

When the image from the passport and the image taken by the camera are compared, these key positions on the face determine whether or not the two images represent the same face.

# Application of 3D scanning – computed tomographic (CT) scanners

COMPUTED TOMOGRAPHIC (CT) SCANNERS are used to create a 3D image of a solid object. This is based on TOMOGRAPHY technology which basically builds up an image of the solid object through a series of very thin 'slices'. Together these 2D 'slices' make up a representation of the 3D solid object.

Each slice is built up by use of X-rays, radio frequencies or gamma imaging; although a number of other methods exist. Each 'slice' is then stored as a digital image in the computer memory. The whole of the solid object is represented digitally in the computer memory.

Depending on how the image is formed, the type of tomographic scanner can have different names. For example:

- X-rays          CT scanners    computerised tomography
- radio frequencies    MRI        magnetic resonance imaging
- gamma rays       SPECT      single photon emission computed tomography.

Figure 5.3 shows a simple example of how tomography works.

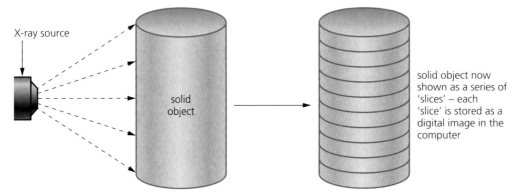

Figure 5.3

## 5.2.2 Barcode readers/scanners

A barcode is a series of dark and light parallel lines of varying thickness. The numbers 0 to 9 are each represented by a unique series of lines. Various barcode methods for representing these digits exist. The example we shall use adopts different codes for digits appearing on the left and for digits appearing on the right (known as UPC (Universal Product Code) version A).

The actual left-hand and right-hand sides of the barcode are separated using guard bars. The structure of these guard bars is shown in Figure 5.4. Figure 5.5 is an example of a barcode showing the left-hand side and right-hand side and the three sets of guard bars.

Each digit is represented by bars of 1 to 4 blocks thick as shown in Figure 5.6.

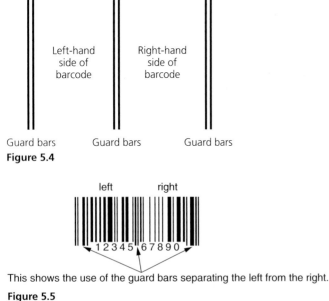

Figure 5.4

Figure 5.5

This shows the use of the guard bars separating the left from the right.

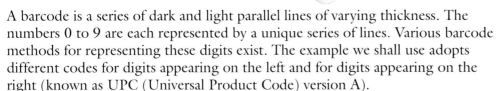

Figure 5.6

The barcode to represent the number 5 4 3 0 5 2 would therefore be as shown in Figure 5.7.

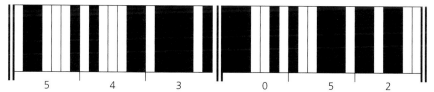

**Figure 5.7**

Each digit is made up of two dark lines and two light lines. The width representing each digit is the same, thus the speed of scanning isn't important. The digits on the left have an odd number of dark elements and always begin with a light bar; the digits on the right have an even number of dark elements and always begin with a dark bar. This arrangement allows a barcode to be scanned in any direction.

## Activity 5.1

a Using the data in Figure 5.6, design the barcodes for:
  i 9 0 0 3 4 0 (three digits on the left; three digits on the right)
  ii 1 2 5 7 6 6 4 8 (four digits on the left; four digits on the right)
  iii 0 5 8 8 9 0 2 9 1 8 (five digits on the left; five digits on the right).
b Look at some barcodes on a variety of products and see how many fit the above system; for those that don't, try to draw up a table similar to that in Figure 5.6 to show the barcode for each digit.

So what happens when a barcode is scanned?

- The barcode is first read by a red laser or red **LED** (LIGHT EMITTING DIODE).
- Light is reflected back off the barcode; the dark areas reflect little or no light which allows the bars to be read.
- The reflected light is read by sensors (photoelectric cells).
- As the laser or LED light is scanned across the barcode, a pattern is generated which is converted into digital data – this allows the computer to understand the barcode.
- For example: the digit '3' on the left generates the pattern **L D D D D L D** (where L = light and D = dark); this has the binary equivalent of **0 1 1 1 1 0 1** (where **L = 0** and **D = 1**).

Barcode readers are most commonly found at the checkout in supermarkets. There are several other input and output devices at the checkout:

**Table 5.1**

| Input/output device | How it is used |
| --- | --- |
| keypad | to key in the number of same items bought; to key in a weight; to key in the number under the barcode if it cannot be read by the barcode reader/scanner |
| screen/monitor | to show the cost of an item and other information |
| speaker | to make a beeping sound every time a barcode is read correctly; but also to make another sound if there is an error when reading the barcode |
| printer | to print out a receipt/itemised list |
| magnetic stripe reader | to read the customer's credit/debit card |
| touchscreen | to select items by touching an icon (such as fresh fruit which may be sold loose without packaging) |

So the barcode has been read, then what happens?

- The barcode number is looked up in the stock database (the barcode is known as the KEY FIELD in the stock item record); this key field uniquely identifies each stock item.
- When the barcode number is found, the stock item record is looked up.
- The price and other stock item details are sent back to the checkout (or POINT OF SALE TERMINAL (POS)).
- The number of stock items in the record is reduced by one each time the barcode is read.
- This new value for number of stock items is written back to the stock item record.
- The number of stock items is compared to the re-order level; if it is less than or equal to this value, more stock items are *automatically* ordered.
- Once an order for more stock items is generated, a flag is added to the record to stop re-ordering every time the stock item barcode is read.
- When new stock items arrive, the stock levels are updated in the database.

Advantages of using barcodes to the management include:

- much easier and faster to change prices on stock items
- much better, more up-to-date sales information/sales trends
- no need to price every stock item on the shelves (this reduces time and cost to the management)
- allows for automatic stock control
- possible to check customer buying habits more easily by linking barcodes to, for example, customer loyalty cards.

Advantages of using barcodes to the customers include:

- faster checkout queues (staff don't need to remember/look up prices of items)
- errors in charging customers are reduced
- the customer is given an itemised bill
- cost savings can be passed on to the customer
- better track of 'sell by dates' so food should be fresher.

The barcode system is used in many other areas. For example, it can be utilised in libraries where barcodes are used in books and on the borrower's library card. Every time a book is taken out, the borrower is linked to the book automatically. This allows automatic checking of when the book is due to be returned, for example.

## Activity 5.2
Find out more about how barcodes can be used in a library. Consider the types of files needed and how the system can track where books are in the library, which books are out on loan, which customer has borrowed a book and so on.

## Activity 5.3
Carry out some research and find out about as many different barcode applications as you can. Try to find out why barcodes are used in each application and determine the advantage of using this type of technology.

### 5.2.3 Quick response (QR) codes

Another type of barcode is the QUICK RESPONSE (QR) CODE. This is made up of a matrix of filled-in dark squares on a light background.

For example, the QR code in Figure 5.8 contains the message: 'computer science textbook – CIE syllabus'.

To make a comparison, normal barcodes (as described in Section 5.2.2) can hold up to 30 digits; QR codes can hold over 7000 digits. This obviously gives greater scope for the storage of information.

Because of modern smart phones, which allow internet access on the move, QR codes can be scanned anywhere. This allows advertising of products on trains, buses, shopping malls and many other places. By using the built-in camera facility on modern phones and downloading the appropriate application (or app), it is possible to read the QR code. The code may contain a website link or some form of advertising (e.g. special offers on pizzas).

Figure 5.8

For example, the QR code in Figure 5.9 contains a phone number and an advertisement for free pizzas if ordered today. On scanning the QR code, the phone number and advertisement will appear on the mobile phone's screen. Advantages of QR codes include:

Figure 5.9

- there is no need for the user to write down or key in a website address; scanning the QR code does this automatically
- QR codes can store website addresses/URLs that appear in magazines, trains, buses or even on business cards, giving a very effective method of advertising.

### 5.2.4 Digital cameras

Digital cameras have essentially replaced the more traditional camera that used film to record the photos. The film required developing and then printing before the photographer could see the result of their work. This made these cameras expensive to operate since it wasn't possible to delete unwanted photographs.

Modern digital cameras simply link to a computer system via a USB port or by using Bluetooth (which enables wireless transfer of photographic files).

These cameras are controlled by a microprocessor which can automatically carry out the following tasks:

- adjust the shutter speed
- focus the image automatically
- operate the flash automatically
- adjust the aperture size
- adjust the size of the image
- remove 'red eye' when the flash has been used

and so on.

Figure 5.10 Digital camera

The photograph is captured when light passes through the lens onto a light-sensitive cell. This cell is made up of tiny elements known as pixels. The number of pixels determines the size of the file used to store the photograph (e.g. a 14-megapixel camera will need 42 megabytes to store each raw (uncompressed) photograph). By reducing the resolution to, for example, a jpeg image, the storage requirement is reduced to 4 megabytes (see Section 6.2.3). The quality of the photograph also depends on many other factors, such as:

- the type of lens used
- the lighting

and so on.

Mobile phones have caught up with digital cameras as regards number of pixels. The drawback is usually poor lens quality and limited memory for the storage of photos. But this may all change in the next few years.

## 5.2.5 Keyboards

Keyboards are by far the most common method used for data entry. They are used as the input device on computers, tablets, mobile phones and many other electronic items.

The keyboard is connected to the computer either by using a USB connection or by wireless connection. In the case of tablets and mobile phones, the keyboard is often VIRTUAL or a type of TOUCHSCREEN technology.

As explained in Chapter 1, each character on a keyboard has an ASCII value. Each character pressed is converted into a digital signal, which the computer interprets.

Keyboards are a relatively slow method of data entry and are also prone to errors. But they are probably still the easiest way to enter text into a computer. However, frequent use of these devices can lead to injuries, such as REPETITIVE STRAIN INJURY (RSI) in the hands and wrists.

Ergonomic keyboards can help to overcome this problem – these have the keys arranged differently as shown in Figure 5.12. They are also designed to give more support to the wrists and hands when doing a lot of typing.

**Figure 5.11** Keyboard

**Figure 5.12** Ergonomic keyboard

## 5.2.6 Pointing devices

The selection of an application often requires the user to 'click' on an icon. Selection of the icon is usually done with a POINTING DEVICE (such as a MOUSE or a TRACKERBALL) or by using a touchscreen.

The mouse is probably still the most common pointing device and comes in various forms:

- the more traditional type with a mechanical ball arrangement; connected to the computer through a USB port
- the more modern type that use red LEDs to detect movement in the $x$-$y$ direction; these are a type of optical mouse
- mice that use either of the above types of technology but use a wireless connection to the computer.

**Figure 5.13** Trackerball

Whatever type of mouse is used it will require an area of desk space to allow movement. They often require a mouse mat since some surfaces, such as paper, prevent the correct operation of the device. Depending on the type of computer, the mouse is fitted with one or two buttons to allow for selection and other functions. Many designs of mouse have a scroll wheel to allow rapid movement up and down the screen.

Trackerballs are seen more often in an industrial environment – such as a control room. Because they don't need to move, the trackerball doesn't need any desk space or special surface. The operator is also less likely to suffer from injuries such as RSI. A ball on the top of the trackerball is moved to control a cursor on the screen. As with the mouse, buttons are used to select icons and to carry out other functions.

Most laptop computers have a built-in TOUCH PAD. This contains a tactile sensor which allows the user to control a cursor by simply moving a finger over the surface of the pad. Buttons to the left and right of the pad act in the same way as buttons on a mouse. However, by simply tapping the surface this acts as a quick method of selection on many touch pads.

## 5.2.7 Microphones

**Microphones** are used to input sound to a computer. For example:

- doing a 'voice over' in a presentation
- part of a speech recognition system
- part of a voice recognition system
- enabling a disabled person to communicate with a computer.

**Microphones** are either built into the computer or are external devices connected through the USB port or using wireless connectivity.

When a microphone picks up sound, a diaphragm vibrates producing an electric signal. This signal goes to a sound card and is converted into digital values and stored in the computer.

If the microphone is being used in a VOICE RECOGNITION system, the user's voice is detected and then converted into digital. A few words spoken produce a digital wave pattern. Software compares this wave pattern to wave patterns stored in memory to see if they match. If they match, then the person has been correctly identified. Only certain words can be used since the system is designed to recognise only a few key phrases (e.g. a user may be asked to say their name). This technology can be used in security systems.

SPEECH RECOGNITION is a different and more complex technology. This again uses a microphone to input words spoken by a user. But this time the software doesn't try to recognise the person talking. The spoken words are recognised and shown on a screen, input into a word processor or used in other application. The basic differences to voice recognition are described below.

**Figure 5.14** Microphone

1 Suppose a person says the word 'HUT'; the sound card in the computer will convert the sound wave into a digital form:

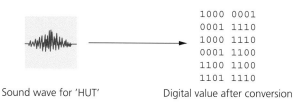

```
1000 0001
0001 1110
1000 1110
0001 1100
1100 1100
1101 1110
```

Sound wave for 'HUT'          Digital value after conversion

**Figure 5.15**

2 The software takes the digital image (shown in Figure 5.15) and breaks it up into phonemes (these are the smallest elements that make up a language); in this case 'H UH T'.

3 These phonemes are compared with words found in the built-in dictionary:

```
                    H A N G
                    H U N G
H UH T  ──────▶     H U N T
                    H U R T
                    H U T
```

**Figure 5.16**

4 The word 'HUT' would then be suggested by the software in whatever application is being run.

5 This, of course, is a very simple example and the whole concept of speech recognition is very complex. In trying to recognise which words are being spoken, the software has to take into account different dialects, different accents and so on. Just to indicate how difficult this is, consider the following well-known example:

The two phrases: 'recognise speech' and 'wreak a nice beach', if spoken quickly, are almost identical. Using phonemes, they become:
'r eh k ao g n ay z / s p iy ch' and 'r eh k / ay / n ay s / b iy ch'

One way round this is to 'train' the computer to understand a cross-section of people; but some problems are difficult to resolve. Human beings have problems with dialects and accents; so it should come as no surprise that this continues to challenge the software developers of speech recognition systems.

## Activity 5.4
Describe how speech recognition could be used to:

a teach language skills to people who have difficulty in learning
b teach a person to say words in a foreign language.

Both voice recognition and speech recognition can be used in various other applications. For example, voice recognition is used in cars to allow the driver to say commands: 'make warmer', 'switch on GPS' or 'open window'. Key words have to be used so that the software can compare voice patterns with the limited dictionary of words already stored. These systems are becoming increasingly sophisticated so that normal speech in the car doesn't trigger an unwanted response by the computer. Newer systems can also be set up to only respond to commands from the driver.

## Activity 5.5
Consider the pluses and minuses of using voice recognition in a car. Is it safer? For example, it may allow a driver to respond to an email while driving etc. Try to develop this argument and draw a valid conclusion from your findings.

## 5.2.8 Touchscreens

Touchscreens are now a very common form of input device. They allow simple touch to launch an application or to carry out many of the functions of pointing devices such as a mouse.

One of the main uses of touchscreen technology is in mobile phones. At present, there are three major types of touchscreen technologies applied to mobile phone screens:

- capacitive
- infra-red
- resistive.

We will consider how each of these technologies work and what their main benefits and drawbacks are.

**CAPACITIVE**

- This is made up of many layers of glass that act like a capacitor, creating electric fields between the glass plates in layers.
- When the top glass layer is touched, the electric current changes and the coordinates where the screen was touched is determined by an on-board microprocessor.

**Benefits**

- This is a medium cost technology.
- Screen visibility is good even in strong sunlight.
- It permits multi-touch capability.
- The screen is very durable; it takes a major impact to break the glass.

**Drawbacks**

- Allows only the use of bare fingers as the form of input; although the latest screens permit a special stylus to be used.

**Figure 5.17**

**INFRA-RED (heat and optical)**

| Heat-sensitive | Optical |
|---|---|
| - Uses glass as the screen material.<br>- Needs a warm object (e.g. fingers) to carry out an input operation. | - Uses glass as the screen material.<br>- Uses an array of sensors (in the form of a grid); the point of contact is based on which grid coordinate is touched. |

**Benefits**

- Both systems allow multi-touch capabilities.
- The optical system allows the use of bare fingers, gloved fingers or a stylus for input.
- Both systems have good screen durability; it take a major impact to break the glass.

**Drawbacks**

- It is relatively expensive technology.
- Heat-sensitive system only allows bare fingers to be used for input (gloved fingers or stylus don't work).
- Both systems (optical and heat-sensitive) have fairly good screen visibility in strong sunlight.

**Figure 5.18**

**RESISTIVE**

- This makes use of an upper layer of polyester (a form of plastic) and a bottom layer of glass.
- When the top polyester layer is touched, the top layer and the bottom layer complete a circuit.
- Signals are then sent out which are interpreted by a microprocessor, the calculations determine the coordinates of where the screen was touched.

**Benefits**

- It is relatively inexpensive technology.
- It is possible to use bare fingers, gloved fingers or a stylus to carry out an input operation.

**Drawbacks**

- Screen visibility is poor in strong sunlight.
- It doesn't permit multi-touch capability.
- The screen durability is only fair; it is vulnerable to scratches and the screen wears out through time.

**Figure 5.19**

## 5.2.9 Sensors

**SENSORS** are devices which read or measure physical properties. These can include temperature, pressure, acidity and so on. Real data is **ANALOGUE** in nature – this means it is constantly changing and doesn't have a discrete value. Analogue data usually requires some form of interpretation; for example, the temperature measurement on a mercury thermometer requires the user to look at the height of the mercury to work out the temperature. The temperature can therefore have an infinite number of values depending on the precision of how the height of the mercury is measured. Equally an analogue clock face requires the user to look at the hands on the clock face. The area swept out by the hands allows the number of hours and minutes to be interpreted. There are many other examples.

However, computers cannot make any sense of these physical quantities and the data needs to be converted into a digital format. This is usually achieved by an ANALOGUE TO DIGITAL CONVERTER (**ADC**). This device converts physical values into discrete digital values.

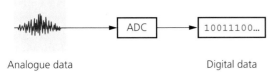

Analogue data                          Digital data

**Figure 5.20**

When the computer is used to control devices, such as a motor or a valve, it is necessary to use a DIGITAL TO ANALOGUE CONVERTER (**DAC**) since these devices need analogue data to operate in many cases. Frequently, an ACTUATOR is used in these control applications. Although these are technically output devices, they are mentioned here since they are an integral part of the control system. An actuator is an electromechanical device such as a relay, solenoid or motor. Note that a solenoid is an example of a digital actuator; part of the device is connected to a computer which opens and closes a circuit as required. When energised, the solenoid may operate a plunger or armature to control, for example, a fuel injection system. Other actuators, such as motors and valves, may require a DAC so that they receive an electric current rather than a simple digital signal direct from the computer.

Table 5.2 shows a number of common sensors and examples of applications that use the named sensors.

**Table 5.2**

| Sensor | Application |
|---|---|
| temperature | • control a central heating system<br>• control/monitor a chemical process<br>• control/monitor the temperature in a greenhouse |
| moisture/humidity | • control/monitor the moisture levels in soil in a greenhouse<br>• control/monitor the humidity levels in the air in a greenhouse<br>• monitor dampness levels in an industrial application (e.g., monitor moisture in a paint spray booth in a car factory) |
| light | • switch street lighting on at night and off during the day<br>• monitor/control light levels in a greenhouse<br>• automatically switch on a car's headlights when it gets dark |
| infra-red/motion | • turn on the windscreen wipers on a car automatically<br>• detect intruders in a burglar alarm system<br>• count people entering/leaving a building |
| pressure | • detect intruders in a burglar alarm system<br>• weigh things (e.g. check the weight of a vehicle)<br>• monitor/control a process where gas pressure is important |
| acoustic/sound | • pick up noise levels (e.g. footsteps) in a burglar alarm system<br>• detect the noise of liquids dripping in a pipe |
| gas (e.g. $O_2$ or $CO_2$) | • monitor pollution levels in a river or in the air<br>• measure $O_2$ and $CO_2$ levels in a greenhouse<br>• check for $CO_2$ leaks in a power station |
| pH | • monitor/control acidity/alkalinity levels in the soil in a greenhouse<br>• pollution/environmental monitoring in rivers |
| magnetic field | • any application where detection of changes in a magnetic field is required (e.g. in cell phones, CD players, etc.)<br>• used in anti-lock braking systems in motor vehicles |

Sensors are used in both monitoring and control applications. There is a subtle difference between how these two methods work:

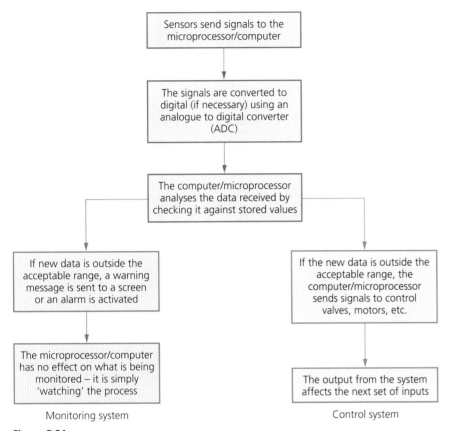

Figure 5.21

Examples of monitoring include:

- monitoring a patient in a hospital for vital signs such as heart rate, temperature, etc.
- monitoring of intruders in a burglar alarm system
- checking the temperature levels in a car engine
- monitoring pollution levels in a river.

Examples of control include:

- turning street lights on at night and turning them off again during daylight
- regulating the temperature in a central heating/air conditioning system
- changing the traffic lights at a road junction
- operating anti-lock brakes on a car when necessary
- regulating the environment in a greenhouse.

# 5.2.10 Monitoring applications

## Burglar alarm system

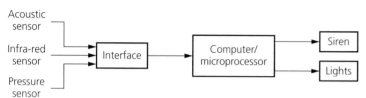

**Figure 5.22**

A burglar alarm monitoring system will carry out the following actions:

- The system is activated by keying in a password on a keypad.
- The infra-red sensor picks up the movement of an intruder in the building.
- The acoustic sensor picks up sounds such as footsteps or breaking glass.
- The pressure sensor picks up the weight of an intruder coming through a door or through a window.
- The sensor data is passed through an ADC if it is in an analogue form to produce digital data.
- The computer/microprocessor will sample the digital data coming from these sensors at a given frequency (e.g. every five seconds); the data is compared with the stored values by the computer/microprocessor.
- If any of the incoming data values are outside the acceptable range, then the computer sends a signal to:
  - a siren to sound the alarm, or
  - a light to start flashing.
- A DAC is used if the devices need analogue values to operate them.
- The alarm continues to sound/lights continue to flash until the system is reset with a password.

## Monitoring of patients in a hospital

- A number of sensors are attached to the patient; these measure vital signs such as: temperature, heart rate, breathing rate, etc.
- These sensors are all attached to a computer system.
- The sensors constantly send data back to the computer system.
- The computer samples the data at frequent intervals.
- The range of acceptable values for each parameter is keyed in to the computer.
- The computer compares the values from the sensors with those values keyed in.
- If anything is out of the acceptable range, a signal is sent by the computer to sound an alarm.
- If data from the sensors is within range, the values are shown in either graphical form on a screen and/or a digital read out.
- Monitoring continues until the sensors are disconnected from the patient.

# 5.2.11 Control applications

## Control of street lighting

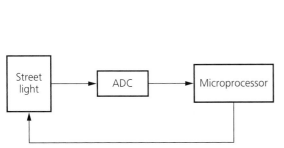

**Figure 5.23**

**Figure 5.24**

This next sequence shows how a microprocessor is used to control the operation of a street lamp. The lamp is fitted with a light sensor which constantly sends data to the microprocessor. The data value from the sensor changes according to whether it is sunny, cloudy, raining or it is night time etc.

- The light sensor sends data to the ADC interface.
- This digitises the data and sends it to the microprocessor.
- The microprocessor samples the data every minute (or at some other frequency rate).
- If the data from the sensor < value stored in memory:
  - a signal is sent from the microprocessor to the street lamp
  - and the lamp is switched on.
- The lamp stays switched on for 30 minutes before the sensor readings are sampled again (this prevents the lamp flickering off and on during brief heavy cloud cover, for example).
- If the data from the sensor >= value stored in memory:
  - a signal is sent from the microprocessor to the street lamp
  - and the lamp is switched off.
- The lamp stays switched off for 30 minutes before sensor readings are sampled again (this prevents the lamp flickering off and on during heavy cloud cover, for example).

## Activity 5.6

Draw a flow diagram to show the steps in how a microprocessor controls the switching off and on of a street lamp. Remember to include a method to stop the lamp switching on and off every few seconds.

## Anti-lock braking systems (on cars)

**ANTI-LOCK BRAKING SYSTEMS (ABS)** on cars use magnetic field sensors to stop the wheels locking up on the car if the brakes have been applied too sharply.

- When one of the car wheels rotates too slowly (i.e. it is locking up), a magnetic field sensor sends data to a microprocessor.
- The microprocessor checks the rotation speed of the other three wheels.
- If they are different (i.e. rotating faster), the microprocessor sends a signal to the braking system:

- and the braking pressure to the affected wheel is reduced
- the wheel's rotational speed is then increased to match the other wheels.
- Checking the rotational speed using these magnetic field sensors is done several times a second and the braking pressure to all the wheels can be constantly changing to prevent any of the wheels locking up under heavy braking; this is felt as a 'judder' on the brake pedal as the braking system is constantly switched off and on to equalise the rotational speed of all four wheels.
- If one of the wheels is rotating too quickly, braking pressure is increased to that wheel until it matches the other three.

### Activity 5.7
Find out more details about how the ABS system works and how it is modified in modern systems such as traction control.
Investigate other uses of magnetic field sensors.

## 5.2.12 Interactive whiteboards

Interactive whiteboards are devices that allow computer images to be displayed on a whiteboard using a digital projector. They also allow a user to write on the whiteboard and the text or drawings produced are then stored in an electronic form for later use. Basically the information which is hand-drawn or hand-written can be stored so nothing from, for example, a meeting is lost.

Suppose a new car has been designed and its image has been projected onto the whiteboard from a computer-stored file. It is possible for this image to be annotated by adding labels, a description or even changes to the design for later use. The annotated version can then be saved in an electronic form to allow these changes to be made.

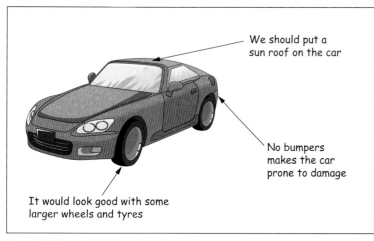

We should put a sun roof on the car

The car and all of the comments and annotations shown would be stored (in a file) so that all of the information at the meeting would be automatically captured

No bumpers makes the car prone to damage

It would look good with some larger wheels and tyres

**Figure 5.25**

It is also possible to run software on the whiteboard and users can interact by simply using their fingers on the whiteboard surface. This allows the user to demonstrate all of the features of the software to, for example, a group of people at a meeting or even a demonstration of a new game in a shopping mall. Any application that runs on a computer can be used on an interactive whiteboard. It is even possible to surf the net, annotate a spreadsheet or demonstrate a drawing package, for example, in real time. The whole audience can see what is happening and even become actively involved in the demonstration.

## 5.3  Output devices

### 5.3.1 Inkjet printers

INKJET PRINTERS are essentially made up of:

- a print head which consists of nozzles which spray droplets of ink on to the paper to form characters
- an ink cartridge or cartridges; either a group of cartridges for each colour (blue, yellow and magenta) and a black cartridge or one single cartridge containing all three colours + black (Note: some systems use six colours.)
- a stepper motor and belt which moves the print head assembly across the page from side to side
- a paper feed which automatically feeds the printer with pages as they are required.

The ink droplets are produced currently using two different technologies.

**Figure 5.26** Inkjet printer

- Thermal bubble: tiny resistors create localised heat which makes the ink vaporise. This causes the ink to form a tiny bubble; as the bubble expands, some of the ink is ejected from the print head onto the paper. When the bubble collapses, a small vacuum is created which allows fresh ink to be drawn into the print head. This continues until the printing cycle is completed.
- Piezoelectric: a crystal is located at the back of the ink reservoir for each nozzle. The crystal is given a tiny electric charge which makes it vibrate. This vibration forces ink to be ejected onto the paper; at the same time more ink is drawn in for further printing.

When a user wishes to print a document using an inkjet printer, the following sequence of events takes place. Whatever technology is used, the basic steps in the printing process are the same.

**Table 5.3**

| Stage in process | Description of what happens |
|---|---|
| 1 | The data from the document is sent to a printer driver |
| 2 | The printer driver ensures that the data is in a format that the chosen printer can understand |
| 3 | A check is made by the printer driver to ensure that the chosen printer is available to print (e.g. is it busy, is it off line, is it out of ink, and so on) |
| 4 | The data is then sent to the printer and it is stored in a temporary memory known as a printer buffer (see Section 4.3) |
| 5 | A sheet of paper is then fed into the main body of the printer; a sensor detects whether paper is available in the paper feed tray – if it is out of paper (or the paper is jammed) then an error message is sent back to the computer |
| 6 | As the sheet of paper is fed through the printer, the print head moves from side to side across the paper printing the text or image; the four ink colours are sprayed in their exact amounts to produce the desired final colour |
| 7 | At the end of each full pass of the print head, the paper is advanced very slightly to allow the next line to be printed; this continues until the whole page has been printed |
| 8 | If there is more data in the printer buffer, then the whole process from stage 5 is repeated until the buffer is finally empty |
| 9 | Once the printer buffer is empty, the printer sends an interrupt (see Section 4.3) to the processor in the computer; this is a request for more data to be sent to the printer; the whole process continues until the whole of the document has been printed |

## 5.3.2 Laser printers

LASER PRINTERS differ greatly from inkjet printers in the way they print pages. They use dry powder ink rather than liquid ink and make use of the properties of static electricity to produce the text and images. Unlike inkjet printers, laser printers print the whole page in one go (inkjet printers print the page line by line).

Their advantage is the speed at which they can carry out large print jobs (e.g. 2000 leaflets) and the fact that they don't run out of ink halfway through.

The following table describes briefly the stages that occur when a document is printed using a laser printer:

**Figure 5.27** Laser printer

**Table 5.4**

| Stage in process | Description of what happens |
|---|---|
| 1 | The data from the document is sent to a printer driver |
| 2 | The printer driver ensures that the data is in a format that the chosen printer can understand |
| 3 | A check is made by the printer driver to ensure that the chosen printer is available to print (e.g. is it busy, is it off line, is it out of ink, and so on) |
| 4 | The data is then sent to the printer and it is stored in a temporary memory known as a printer buffer (refer to Section 4.3 for more details) |
| 5 | The start of the printing process involves a printing drum being given a positive charge; as this drum rotates, a laser beam is scanned across it removing the positive charge in certain areas; this leaves negatively charged areas which exactly match the text/images of the page to be printed |
| 6 | The drum is then coated with positively charged TONER (powdered ink); since the toner is positively charged, it only sticks to the negatively charged parts of the drum |
| 7 | A negatively charged sheet of paper is then rolled over the drum |
| 8 | The toner on the drum now sticks to the paper to produce an exact copy of the page sent to the printer |
| 9 | To prevent the paper sticking to the drum, the electric charge on the paper is removed after one rotation of the drum |
| 10 | The paper finally goes through a fuser which is a set of heated rollers; the heat melts the ink so that it fixes permanently to the paper |
| 11 | At the very end, a discharge lamp removes all the electric charge from the drum making it ready to print the next page |

## Applications of inkjet and laser printers

The choice of whether to use an inkjet printer or laser printer depends on which features make it the most appropriate output device for the given application.

INKJET PRINTERS are best for one-off photos or where only a few pages of good quality, colour printing are needed; the small ink cartridges or small paper trays would not be an issue with such applications.

LASER PRINTERS produce high quality printouts and are very fast when making multiple copies of a document; any application that needs high-volume printing (in colour or monochrome) would choose the laser printer (for example, producing a large number of high quality flyers or posters for advertising) – they have two advantages: they have large toner cartridges and large paper trays (often holding more than a ream of paper).

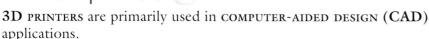

**Activity 5.8**
Find out how the operation of colour laser printers differs from the operation of monochrome laser printers.

## 5.3.3 3D printers

**3D PRINTERS** are primarily used in COMPUTER-AIDED DESIGN **(CAD)** applications.

They can produce solid objects which actually work. The solid object is built up layer by layer (refer to Section 5.2.1 for more details) using materials such as powdered resin, powdered metal, paper or ceramic powder.

The motorcycle in Figure 5.29 was made using an industrial 3D printer. It was made from many layers (0.1 mm thick) of powdered metal using a technology known as BINDER **3D PRINTING.**

The following describes some of the features of 3D printing:

**Figure 5.28** 3D printer

- Various types of 3D printers exist; they range from the size of a microwave oven up to the size of a small car.
- 3D printers use ADDITIVE manufacturing (i.e. the object is built up layer by layer); this is in sharp contrast to the more traditional method of SUBTRACTIVE manufacturing (i.e. removal of material to make the object). For example, making a statue using a 3D printer would involve building it up layer by layer using powdered stone until the final object was formed. The subtractive method would involve carving the statue out of solid stone (i.e. removing the stone not required) until the final item was produced. Similarly, **CNC** machining removes metal to form an object; 3D printing would produce the same item by building up the object from layers of powdered metal.

**Figure 5.29** Motorcycle

- **Direct 3D printing** uses inkjet technology; a print head can move left to right as in a normal printer. However, the print head can also move up and down to build up the layers of an object.
- **Binder 3D printing** is similar to direct 3D printing. However, this method uses two passes for each of the layers; the first pass sprays dry powder and then on the second pass a binder (a type of glue) is sprayed to form a solid layer.
- Newer technologies are using lasers and UV light to harden liquid polymers; this further increases the diversity of products which can be made.

## How to create a solid object using a 3D printer

There are a number of steps in the process of producing an object using these 3D printers. The steps are summarised in Figure 5.30.

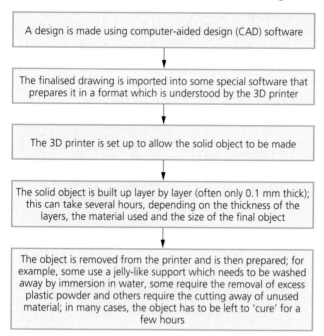

```
A design is made using computer-aided design (CAD) software
        │
        ▼
The finalised drawing is imported into some special software that
prepares it in a format which is understood by the 3D printer
        │
        ▼
The 3D printer is set up to allow the solid object to be made
        │
        ▼
The solid object is built up layer by layer (often only 0.1 mm thick);
this can take several hours, depending on the thickness of the
layers, the material used and the size of the final object
        │
        ▼
The object is removed from the printer and is then prepared; for
example, some use a jelly-like support which needs to be washed
away by immersion in water, some require the removal of excess
plastic powder and others require the cutting away of unused
material; in many cases, the object has to be left to 'cure' for a
few hours
```

**Figure 5.30**

## Uses of 3D printing

3D printing is regarded as being possibly the next 'industrial revolution' since it will change the manufacturing methods in many industries. The following list is just a glimpse into what we know can be made using these printers; in the years to come, this list will probably fill an entire book:

- prosthetic limbs made to exactly fit the recipient
- items to allow precision reconstructive surgery (e.g. facial reconstruction following an accident); the parts made by this technique are more precise in their design since they are made from exact scanning of the skull
- in aerospace, manufacturers are looking at making wings and other parts using 3D technology; the bonus will be lightweight precision parts
- in fashion and art – 3D printing allows new creative ideas to be developed
- making parts for items no longer in production, e.g. suspension parts for a vintage car.

These are just a few of the exciting applications which make use of this new technology.

> ### Activity 5.9
> Do a search on the internet to find new and innovative 3D printer applications.
> Have a class discussion on how these printers could herald the start of a new 'industrial revolution'.

### 5.3.4 2D and 3D cutters

A three-dimensional (3D) laser cutter works in a similar way to a two-dimensional (2D) cutter. The main difference is that the 3D cutter can recognise an object in the *x-y-z* direction rather than just *x-y*.

3D laser cutters can cut the following materials:

- glass
- crystal
- metal
- polymer
- wood.

Very complex designs can be cut since the cutters are controlled by computers and very sophisticated software.

A 3D cutter can cut beyond the surface of the material and produce very intricate designs.

It is interesting to contrast this method of shaping objects with 3D printers, although it is true to say that not all the materials which can undergo 3D cutting can be used in 3D printing methods.

### 5.3.5 Actuators

These are covered in detail in Section 5.2.9. ACTUATORS are used in many control applications involving sensors and devices such as ADC and DAC.

### 5.3.6 Loudspeakers/headphones

Sound is produced from a computer by passing the digital data through a DIGITAL TO ANALOGUE CONVERTER (**DAC**) and then through an AMPLIFIER; finally the sound emerges from a (loud)SPEAKER.

The sound is produced by voltage differences vibrating a cone in the speaker housing at different frequencies and amplitudes:

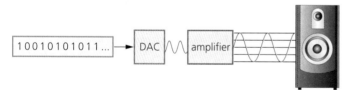

**Figure 5.31**

The rate at which the DAC can translate the digital output into analogue voltages is known as the SAMPLING RATE. If the DAC is a 16-bit device, then it can accept numbers between +32 767 ($2^{16}$ – 1) and –32 768 ($2^{16}$); the digital value containing all zeros is ignored. The speed at which these values can be converted is the sampling rate.

Most textbooks indicate that the standard sampling rate is 44 100 samples per second. This basically means that the the DAC can convert 44 100 values in the range +32 767 to –32 768 every second.

Suppose a CD is being produced to contain a number of music tracks. Each piece of music is sampled 44 100 times a second. Each sample is 16 bits. Since the music is in stereo this also needs to be taken into consideration.

The above information means that 44 100 × 2 × 16 = 1 411 200 bits per second sampling (the number '2' is used in the calculation to account for the sound being in stereo).

Since 1 byte = 8 bits, this equates to 1 411 200/8 bytes per second.

This works out at 176 400 bytes per second.

> ### Activity 5.10
> a Calculate how much memory is needed to store a four-minute music track using the number of bytes needed per second from above.
>   Convert your answer into megabytes (using the data from Chapter 1).
> b If the CD has a capacity of 800 megabytes, how many four-minute songs could be stored on the CD?

## 5.3.7 LCD and LED monitors

The days of the old cathode-ray monitors are almost gone. Most monitors and television sets these days are made using LIQUID CRYSTAL DISPLAY/DIODE (**LCD**) technology.

This means that the front layer of the monitor is made up of liquid crystal diodes; these tiny diodes are grouped together in threes or fours which are known as pixels (picture elements). The three colours which are grouped together use red, green and blue diodes. Those systems that use groups of four include a yellow diode – this is said to make the colours more vivid.

Modern LCD monitors are back lit using LIGHT EMITTING DIODE (**LED**) technology. This gives the image better contrast and brightness. Before the use of LEDs, LCD monitors used a cold cathode fluorescent lamp (CCFL) as the backlighting method.

Essentially, CCFL uses two fluorescent tubes behind the LCD screen which supplies the light source. When LEDs are used, a matrix of tiny LEDs is used behind the LCD screen. Because LCD doesn't emit any light, some form of back-lit technology needs to be used.

LEDs have become increasingly more popular because of a number of advantages over older CCFL technology:

- LEDs reach their maximum brightness almost immediately (there is no need to 'warm up' before reaching full efficiency)
- LEDs give a whiter light which sharpens the image and make the colours appear more vivid; CCFL had a slightly yellowish tint
- LEDs produce a brighter light which improves the colour definition
- monitors using LED technology are much thinner than monitors using CCFL technology
- LEDs last almost indefinitely; this makes the technology more reliable and means a more consistent product
- LEDs consume very little power which means they produce less heat as well as using less energy.

Future LED technology is making use of ORGANIC LIGHT EMITTING DIODES (**OLEDs**). These use organic materials (made up of carbon compounds) to create semi-conductors which are very flexible. Organic films are sandwiched between two charged electrodes (one is a metallic CATHODE and the other a glass ANODE). When an electric field is applied to the electrodes they give off light. This means that no form of backlighting is required. This allows for very thin screens.

It also means that there is no longer a need to use LCD technology, since OLED is a self-contained system.

As can be seen in Figure 5.32, OLEDs allow the screen to be curved. This ensures a good picture from any angle.

But the important aspect of the technology is how thin this makes the screen. It is now possible, using OLED technology, to bend screens to any shape. If this is adopted by mobile phone manufacturers, it will be possible to develop phones which can wrap around your wrist – much like a watch strap.

Imagine screens so thin that they can be folded up and placed in your pocket until they are needed. Or how about using folding OLED displays attached to fabrics creating 'smart' clothing (this could be used on outdoor survival clothing where an integrated circuit, mobile phone, GPS receiver and OLED display could all be sewn into the clothing)?

**Figure 5.32**

Advantages of using OLED compared with existing LEDs and LCDs include:

- the plastic, organic layers of an OLED are thinner, lighter and more flexible than the crystal structures used in LEDs or LCDs
- the light-emitting layers of an OLED are lighter; OLED layers can be made from plastic rather than the glass used in LED and LCD screens
- OLEDs give a brighter light than LEDs
- OLEDs do not require backlighting like LCD screens – OLEDs generate their own light
- since OLEDs require no backlighting, they use much less power than LCD screens (most of the LCD power is used to do the backlighting); this is very important in battery-operated devices such as mobile phones
- since OLEDs are essentially plastics, they can be made into large, thin sheets (this means they could be used on large advertising boards in airports, subways, and so on)
- OLEDs have a very large field of view, about 170 degrees, which makes them ideal for use in television sets and for advertising screens.

---

**Activity 5.11**

Carry out some research into OLED technology (there are numerous internet sites to help you) and answer the following questions:

a Why are inkjet printers helping to keep down the cost of OLED screens?
b How are different colours generated using OLED technology?
c How is the brightness of the display controlled?
d OLEDs refresh 1000 times faster than LCDs; why would this be an advantage? Where could it be used to great effect?

LCD/LED screens are used on many hand-held devices with touchscreens, such as mobile phones, tablets and game consoles. The technology behind such screens was discussed at great length in Section 5.2.8.

Modern LCD screens are very thin and very lightweight and are very responsive to touch. Obviously, the new technologies described above will change the way we use these hand-held devices in the very near future.

## 5.3.8 Light projectors

There are two common types of light projector:

- digital light projectors (DLP)
- LCD projectors.

Projectors are used to project computer output onto larger screens or even onto interactive whiteboards. They are often used in presentations and in multimedia applications.

The following two sections describe the basic differences behind these projector technologies.

### Digital Light Projectors (DLP)

The use of millions of micro mirrors on a small DIGITAL LIGHT PROJECTOR (**DLP**) chip is key to how these devices work.

The number of micro mirrors and the way they are arranged on the DLP chip determines the resolution of the digital image. When the micro mirrors tilt towards the light source, they are ON. When the micro mirrors tilt away from the light source, they are OFF. This creates a light or dark pixel on the projection screen. The micro mirrors can switch on or off several thousand times a second creating various grey shades – typically 1024 grey shades can be produced (for example, if the mirror switches on more often than it switches off, it will produce a lighter shade of grey). This is known as the grey scale image.

A bright white light source (e.g. from a xenon bulb) passes through a colour filter on its way to the DLP chip. The white light is split into the primary colours: red, green and blue – the DLP projector can create over 16 million different colours. The ON and OFF states of each micro mirror are linked with colours from the filter to produce the coloured image.

The whole concept is a little like reverse black and white photography. With DLP technology, the grey scales are interpreted as colours rather than grey representing colours as used in photography.

# LCD projectors

These are older technology than DLP. Essentially a high-intensity beam of light passes through an LCD display and then onto a screen. How this works in principle is described below.

- A powerful beam of white light is generated from a bulb or LED inside the projector body.
- This beam of light is then sent to a group of chromatic-coated mirrors; these reflect the light back at different wavelengths.
- When the white light hits these mirrors, the reflected light has wavelengths corresponding to red, green and blue light components.
- These three different coloured light components pass through three LCD screens; these screens show the image to be projected as millions of pixels in a grey scale.
- When the coloured light passes through the LCD screens, a red, green and blue version of the grey image emerges.
- These images are then combined using a special prism to produce a full colour image – this final image consists of millions of colours (each shade of grey in the original image produces a different shade in each of the colour images).
- Finally the image passes through the projector lens onto a screen.

# 6 Memory and data storage

In this chapter you will learn about:

- file formats such as MIDI, MP3 and jpeg
- file compression techniques
- primary, secondary and off-line storage
- magnetic, optical and solid-state media.

## 6.1 Introduction

There are many file formats used to store data, be this text, images or sound, in computer systems. This chapter will consider how file compression is used to save memory when storing different types of files.

All computer systems have primary memory and secondary memory storage. The main technologies used are magnetic, optical and solid state. Storage devices which use each of these technologies will be described later in this chapter, together with a number of applications.

## 6.2 File formats

A number of different file formats are used in computer systems. We will look at the following ones:

- Musical Instrument Digital Interface (MIDI)
- MP3
- MP4
- jpeg
- text and number format.

## 6.2.1 Musical Instrument Digital Interface (MIDI)

MUSICAL INSTRUMENT DIGITAL INTERFACE (**MIDI**) is always associated with the storage of music files. However, MIDI files are not music and don't contain any sounds; they are very different to, for example, MP3 files. MIDI is essentially a communications protocol that allows electronic musical instruments to interact with each other. The MIDI protocol uses 8-bit serial transmission with one start bit and one stop bit, and is therefore asynchronous (see Section 2.2.3).

A MIDI file consists of a list of commands that instruct a device (for example, an electronic organ, sound card in a computer or in a mobile phone) how to produce a particular sound or musical note. Each MIDI command has a specific sequence of bytes. The first byte is the status byte – this informs the MIDI device what function to perform. Encoded in the status byte is the MIDI channel. MIDI operates on 16 different channels, which are numbered 0 to 15.

Examples of MIDI commands include:

- note on/off: this indicates that a key (on an electronic keyboard) has been pressed/released to produce/stop producing a musical note
- key pressure: this indicates how hard the key has been pressed (this could indicate loudness of the music note or whether any vibrato has been used, and so on).

Two additional bytes are required, a PITCH BYTE, which tells the MIDI device which note to play, and a VELOCITY BYTE, which tells the device how loud to play the note. When music or sound is recorded on a computer system, these MIDI messages are saved in a file which is recognised by the file extension .mid.

If this .mid file is played back through a musical instrument, such as an electronic keyboard, the music will be played back in an identical way to the original. The whole piece of music will have been stored as a series of commands but no actual musical notes. This makes it a very versatile file structure, since the same file could be fed back through a different electronic instrument, such as an electric guitar, with different effects to the original. However, to play back through an instrument such as a guitar would need the use of SEQUENCER SOFTWARE, since the MIDI files wouldn't be recognised in their 'raw' form.

Both the electronic instruments and the computer need a MIDI interface to allow them to 'talk' to each other. It was mentioned earlier that the MIDI operates on 16 channels. In fact the computer can send data out on all 16 MIDI channels at the same time. For example, 16 MIDI devices, each set up for a different MIDI channel, could be connected to the computer. Each device could be playing a separate line in a song from the sequencer software, effectively creating an electronic orchestra. This implementation is being used more and more today in the recording studio, by major orchestras and in musical scores used in films.

Because MIDI files don't contain any audio tracks, their size, compared with an MP3 file, is considerably smaller. For example, a 10 megabyte MP3 file only requires about 10 kilobyte file size when using the MIDI format. This makes them ideal for devices where memory is an issue; for example, storing ring tones on a mobile phone.

## 6.2.2 MPEG-3 (MP3) and MPEG-4 (MP4)

**MPEG-3 (MP3)** uses technology known as AUDIO COMPRESSION to convert music and other sounds into an MP3 file format. Essentially, this compression technology will reduce the size of a normal music file by about 90 per cent. For example, an 80 megabyte music CD can be reduced to 8 megabytes using MP3 technology.

MP3 files are used in MP3 players, computers or mobile phones. Files can be downloaded from the internet, or CDs can be converted to MP3 format. The CD files are converted using FILE COMPRESSION software. Whilst the music quality can never match the 'full' version found on a CD, the quality is satisfactory for most general purposes.

But how can the original music file be reduced by 90 per cent whilst still retaining most of the music quality? This is done using file compression algorithms which use PERCEPTUAL MUSIC SHAPING; this essentially removes sounds that the human ear can't hear properly. For example, if two sounds are played at the same time, only the louder one can be heard by the ear, so the softer sound is eliminated. This means that certain parts of the music can be removed without affecting the quality too much.

MP3 files use what is known as a LOSSY FORMAT (see Section 6.3.2) since part of the original file is lost following the compression algorithm. This means that the original file can't be put back together again. However, even the quality of MP3 files can be different since it depends on the BIT RATE – this is the number of bits per second used when creating the file. Bit rates are roughly between 80 and 320 kilobits per second; usually 200 or higher gives a sound quality close to a normal CD.

**MPEG-4 (MP4)** files are slightly different to MP3 files. This format allows the storage of multimedia files rather than just sound. Music, videos, photos and animation can all be stored in the MP4 format. Videos, for example, could be streamed over the internet using the MP4 format without losing any real discernable quality.

## 6.2.3 Joint Photographic Experts Group (jpeg) files

Look at the following five photographs of the same car wheel:

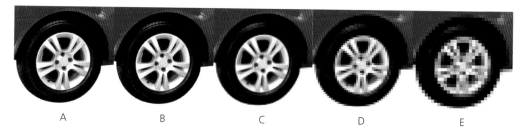

Figure 6.1

The resolution of the photographs is reduced from A to E. Photographs A and B are very sharp whilst photograph D is very fuzzy and E is almost unrecognisable. This is the result of changing the number of PIXELS per centimetre used to store the image (that is, reducing the PICTURE RESOLUTION).

When a photographic file undergoes file compression, the size of the file is reduced. The trade-off for this reduced file size is reduced quality of the image. One of the file formats used to reduce photographic file sizes is known as JPEG. This is another example of lossy file compression. As with MP3 format, once the image is subjected to the jpeg compression algorithm, a new file is formed and the original file can no longer be constructed. Jpeg will reduce the RAW BITMAP image by a factor of between 5 and 15 depending on the quality of the original.

An image that is 2048 pixels wide and 1536 pixels high is equal to $2048 \times 1536$ pixels; in other words, 3 145 728 pixels. This is often referred to as a 3-megapixel image (although it is obviously slightly larger). A raw bitmap can often be referred to as a **TIFF** or **BMP** image (file extension **.TIF** or **.BMP**). The file size of this image is determined by the number of pixels. In the previous example, a 3-megapixel image would be 3 megapixels × 3 colours. In other words, 9 megabytes (each pixel occupies 3 bytes because it is made up of the three main colours: **red**, **green** and **blue**). TIFF and BMP are the highest image quality because, unlike jpeg, they are not in a compressed format.

The same image stored in jpeg format would probably occupy between 0.6 megabytes and 1.8 megabytes.

Jpeg relies on certain properties of the human eye and, up to a point, a certain amount of file compression can take place without any real loss of quality. The human eye is limited in its ability to detect very slight differences in brightness

and in colour hues. For example, some computer imaging software boasts that
it can produce over 40 million different colours – the human eye is only able to
differentiate about 10 million colours.

## Activity 6.2

a  An image is 1200 pixels by 1600 pixels. Calculate:
   i   the total number of pixels in the original image
   ii  the number of bytes occupied by this file
   iii the file size of the jpeg image (in kilobytes) if the original
       image was reduced by a factor of 8.
b  A second image is 3072 pixels by 2304 pixels. Calculate:
   i   the total number of pixels in the original image
   ii  the number of bytes occupied by this file
   iii the file size of the jpeg image (in megabytes) if the original
       image was reduced by a factor of 5.
   iv  How many uncompressed files of the size calculated in part
       (ii) could be stored on a 4-gigabyte memory card?
   v   How many compressed files of the size calculated in part (iii)
       could be stored on the same 4-gigabyte memory card?

## Activity 6.3

The very sharp image A in Figure 6.1 was blown up to about six
times its size:

**Figure 6.2**
Find out why this initially sharp image now appears fuzzy at this
magnification.
How can this problem be overcome?

# 6.2.4 Text and number file formats

Text and numbers can be stored in a number of formats. Text is usually stored in an ASCII format (see Section 1.6.4).

When using spreadsheets or databases, for example, numbers can be stored in a number of different formats:

- real, e.g. 2.71678
- integer, e.g. 3
- date, e.g. 12/08/2016
- time, e.g. 19:45:50
- currency, e.g. R$ 15.50

It is important that the correct format is chosen if some form of processing is to be done. If number files undergo any form of file compression, then it tends to be lossless. Since it is very important that none of the information/data is lost (see Section 6.3).

If ASCII format is used to store text on a file, then the table in Figure 1.7 is used to store each of the characters. For example, the word COMPUTER would be stored as either:

   67 79 77 80 85 84 69 82   or   %43 %4F %4D %50 %55 %54 %45 %52

(the first code is in denary and the second in hexadecimal).

Text files can also undergo file compression. These use complex algorithms that work on redundancy or repeated sections of words (e.g. OU in yOUr, cOUntry or mOUntain). The following section shows, in very simple terms, how this could work:

The phrase 'THIS SECTION SHOWS YOU HOW THIS WOULD WORK' consists of 35 memory units (ignoring spaces). Repeated words, such as 'THIS' could be put into a data dictionary and be replaced by '1'. Repeated word sections, such as 'HOW' and 'OU' could be replaced by the numbers '2' and '3'. Our phrase then becomes '1 SECTION S2S Y3 2 1 W3LD WORK'.

Again, ignoring spaces, this compressed form now uses only 23 memory units. This is about a 33% saving in file size. Obviously if whole pages are to be stored, then repeated words and word sections become even more numerous. Compression algorithms take many things into account when creating these compressed files – but this is outside the scope of this textbook.

This is clearly an example of lossless compression since the original phrase can be reformed if necessary using the data dictionary and compressed file.

# 6.3  Lossless and lossy file compression

## 6.3.1 Lossless file compression

With LOSSLESS FILE COMPRESSION, all the data bits from the original file are reconstructed when the file is again uncompressed. This is particularly important for files where loss of any data would be disastrous – for example, a spreadsheet file.

## 6.3.2 Lossy file compression

LOSSY FILE COMPRESSION is very different to lossless file compression. With this technique, the file compression algorithm eliminates unnecessary bits of data as seen in MP3 and jpeg formats.

It is impossible to get the original file back once it is compressed. This is why it is chosen for files where removing certain bits doesn't detract from the quality.

# 6.4 Memory and storage

Memory and storage devices can be split up into three distinct groups:

- primary memory
- secondary storage
- off-line storage.

Figure 6.3 shows how these all link together:

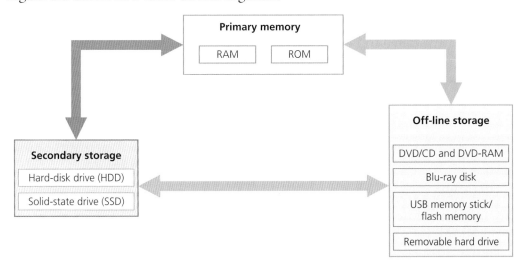

**Figure 6.3**

We will now consider each of the three parts in the diagram.

## 6.4.1 Primary memory

### Random Access Memory (RAM)

The features of **RANDOM ACCESS MEMORY (RAM)** are:

- it is volatile/temporary memory (the contents of the memory are lost when the power to the RAM is turned off)
- it is used to store:
  - data,
  - files, or
  - part of the operating system that are *currently in use*
- it can be written to or read from and the contents of the memory can be changed.

In general, the larger the size of RAM the faster the computer will operate. In reality, the RAM never runs out of memory; it continues to operate but just gets slower and slower. As the RAM becomes full, the processor has to continually access the hard disk drive to overwrite old data on RAM with new data. By increasing the RAM size, the number of times this access operation is carried out is reduced, making the computer run faster.

RAM is much faster to write to or read from than other types of memory; but its main drawback is its volatility.

**Figure 6.4** RAM

Buffers were introduced in Chapter 4 (see Section 4.3). These often use RAM since they need to be a fast memory and the data only needs to be held temporarily. As outlined earlier, buffers allow the processor to do other tasks while slower peripheral devices send data to and receive data from the computer.

There are currently two types of RAM technology:

- dynamic ram (DRAM)
- static RAM (SRAM).

### Dynamic RAM (DRAM)

Each DYNAMIC **RAM (DRAM)** chip consists of a number of transistors and capacitors. Each of these parts is tiny since a single RAM chip will contain millions of transistors and capacitors. The function of each part is:

- capacitor – this holds the bits of information (0 or 1)
- transistor – this acts like a switch; it allows the chip control circuitry to read the capacitor or change the capacitor's value.

This type of RAM needs to be constantly REFRESHED (that is, the capacitor needs to be recharged every 15 microseconds otherwise it would lose its value). If it wasn't refreshed, the capacitor's charge would leak away very quickly, leaving every capacitor with the value 0.

DRAMs have a number of advantages over SRAMs:

**Figure 6.5** DRAM

- they are much less expensive to manufacture than SRAM
- they consume less power than SRAM
- they have a higher storage capacity than SRAM.

### Static RAM (SRAM)

A big difference between SRAM and DRAM is that this type of memory doesn't need to be constantly refreshed.

It makes use of 'flip flops' which hold each bit of memory.

SRAM is much faster than DRAM when it comes to data access (typically, access time for SRAM is 25 nanoseconds and for DRAM is 60 nanoseconds).

DRAM is the most common type of RAM used in computers, but where absolute speed is essential, then SRAM is the preferred technology. For example, the processor's MEMORY CACHE is the high speed portion of the memory; it is effective because most programs access the same data or instructions many times. By keeping as much of this information as possible in SRAM, the computer avoids having to access the slower DRAM.

## Read Only Memory (ROM)

The main features of READ ONLY MEMORY (ROM) can be summarised as follows:

**Figure 6.6** SRAM

- they are non-volatile/permanent memories (the contents of the memory remain even when the power to the ROM is turned off)
- they are often used to store the start-up instructions when the computer is first switched on (for example, ROM might store the basic input/output system (BIOS))
- the data or contents of a ROM chip can only be read; they cannot be changed.

## Application

We will now consider an application, other than a computer, where both RAM and ROM chips are used.

A remote-controlled toy car has a circuitry which contains both RAM and ROM chips. The remote control is a hand-held device.

We will consider the function of each type of memory independently:

- ROM
  - stores the factory settings such as remote control frequencies
  - stores the 'start-up' routines when the toy car is first switched on
  - stores the set routines; for example, how the buttons on the hand-held device control turning left, acceleration, stopping, and so on.
- RAM
  - the user may wish to program in their own routines; these new instructions would be stored in the RAM chip
  - the RAM chip will store the data/instructions received from the remote control unit.

---

### Activity 6.4

Describe how ROM and RAM chips could be used in the following devices:

a  a microwave oven
b  a refrigerator
c  a remote-controlled model aeroplane; the movement of the aeroplane is controlled by a hand-held device.

---

## 6.4.2 Secondary storage

### Hard Disk Drives (HDD)

HARD DISK DRIVES (HDD) are probably still the most common method used to store data on a computer.

Data is stored in a digital format on the magnetic surfaces of the disks (or platters, as they are frequently called). The hard disk drive will have a number of platters which can spin at about 7000 times a second. A number of read–write heads can access all of the surfaces in the disk drive. Normally each platter will have two surfaces which can be used to store the data. These read–write heads can move very quickly – typically they can move from the centre of the disk to the edge of the disk (and back again) 50 times a second.

Data is stored on the surface in sectors and tracks (see Figure 6.8 on next page). A sector on a given track will contain a fixed number of bytes.

Unfortunately, hard disk drives have very slow data access when compared to, for example, RAM. Many applications require the read–write heads to constantly seek for the correct blocks of data; this means a large number of head movements. The effects of LATENCY then become very significant. Latency is defined as the time it takes for a specific block of data on a data track to rotate around to the read–write head.

Users will sometimes notice the effect of latency when they see messages such as 'please wait' or, at its worst, 'not responding'.

**Figure 6.7**

## Solid-state Drives (SSD)

Latency is an issue in HDDs as described earlier. **SOLID-STATE DRIVES (SSD)** remove this issue considerably. They have no moving parts and all data is retrieved at the same rate. They don't rely on magnetic properties; the most common type of solid-state storage devices store data by controlling the movement of electrons within NAND chips. The data is stored as 0s and 1s in millions of tiny transistors within the chip. This effectively produces a non-volatile rewritable memory.

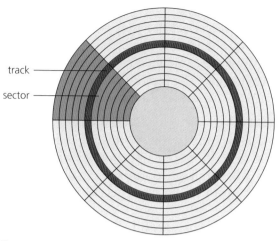

**Figure 6.8**

However, a number of solid-state storage devices sometimes use **ELECTRONICALLY ERASABLE PROGRAMMABLE READ-ONLY MEMORY (EEPROM)** technology. The main difference is the use of NOR chips rather than NAND. This makes them faster in operation but devices using EEPROM are considerably more expensive than those that use NAND technology. EEPROM also allows data to be read or erased in single bytes at a time. Use of NAND only allows blocks of data to be read or erased. This makes EEPROM technology more useful in certain applications where data needs to be accessed or erased in byte-sized chunks.

Because of the cost implications, the majority of solid-state storage devices use NAND technology. The two types are usually distinguished by the terms FLASH (use NAND) and EEPROM (use NOR).

So what are the main benefits of using SSD rather than HDD? The main benefits of SSDs are summarised below:

- they are more reliable (no moving parts to go wrong)
- they are considerably lighter (which makes them suitable for laptops)
- they don't have to 'get up to speed' before they work properly
- they have a lower power consumption
- they run much cooler than HDDs (these last two points again make them very suitable for laptop computers)
- because they have no moving parts, they are very thin
- data access is considerably faster than HDD.

The main drawback of SSD is the questionable longevity of the technology. Most solid state storage devices are conservatively rated at only 20 GB write operations per day over a three-year period – this is known as SSD endurance. For this reason, SSD technology is not used in servers, for example, where a huge number of write operations take place every day. However, this issue is being addressed by a number of manufacturers to improve the durability of these solid-state systems.

# 6.4.3 Off-line storage

Off-line storage includes:

- CD/DVD/DVD-RAM (optical storage systems)
- Blu-ray disks (optical storage systems)
- USB flash memory/memory sticks/SD-XD cards (solid state storage systems)
- removable/external hard disk drives (magnetic storage systems).

# CD/DVD disks

**CDs** and **DVDS** are described as OPTICAL STORAGE DEVICES. Laser light is used to read data and to write data in the surface of the disk.

Both CDs and DVDs use a thin layer of metal alloy or light-sensitive organic dye to store the data. As can be seen in Figure 6.9, both systems use a single, spiral track which runs from the centre of the disk to the edge.

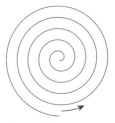

**Figure 6.9**

The data is stored in 'pits' and 'bumps' on the spiral track. A red laser is used to read and write the data. CDs and DVDs can be designated R (write once only) or RW (can be written to or read from many times).

DVD technology is slightly different to that used in CDs. One of the main differences is the use of DUAL-LAYERING which considerably increases the storage capacity. Basically, this means that there are two individual recording layers. Two layers of a standard DVD are joined together with a transparent (polycarbonate) spacer, and a very thin reflector is also sandwiched between the two layers. Reading and writing of the second layer is done by a red laser focusing at a fraction of a millimetre difference compared to the first layer.

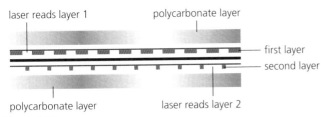

**Figure 6.10**

Standard, single layer DVDs still have a larger storage capacity than CDs because the 'pit' size and track width are both smaller. This means that more data can be stored on the DVD surface. DVDs use lasers with a wavelength of 650 nanometres; CDs use lasers with a wavelength of 780 nanometres. The shorter the wavelength of the laser light, the greater the storage capacity of the medium.

# DVD-RAM

**DVD-RAM** uses a very different technology to CDs and DVDs. They have the following features:

- Instead of a single, spiral track, they use a number of concentric tracks (see Figure 6.11).
- Use of concentric tracks allows simultaneous read and write operations to take place.
- They allow numerous read and write operations (up to 100 000 times) and have great longevity (over 30 years) which makes them ideal for archiving.

**Figure 6.11**

# Blu-ray disks

**BLU-RAY DISKS** are another example of optical storage media. However, they are fundamentally different to DVDs in their construction and in the way they carry out read–write operations.

The main differences are:

- a blue laser, rather than a red laser, is used to carry out read and write operations; the wavelength of blue light is only 405 nanometres (compared to 650 nm for red light)

**Figure 6.12**

- using blue laser light means that the 'pits' and 'bumps' can be much smaller; consequently, Blu-ray can store up to five times more data than normal DVD
- Blu-ray uses a single 1.1 mm thick polycarbonate disk; normal DVDs use a sandwich of two 0.6 mm thick disks
- using two sandwiched layers can cause BIREFRINGENCE (light is refracted into two separate beams causing reading errors); because Blu-ray uses only one layer, the disks don't suffer from birefringence
- Blu-ray disks automatically come with a secure encryption system which helps to prevent piracy and copyright infringement.

Table 6.1 summarises the main differences between CDs, DVDs and Blu-ray.

**Table 6.1**

| Disk type | Laser colour | Wavelength of laser light | Disk construction | Track pitch (distance between tracks) |
|-----------|--------------|---------------------------|-------------------|---------------------------------------|
| CD | red | 780 nm | single 1.2 mm polycarbonate layer | 1.60 μm |
| DVD | red | 650 nm | two 0.6 mm polycarbonate layers | 0.74 μm |
| Blu-ray | blue | 405 nm | single 1.1 mm polycarbonate layer | 0.30 μm |

(Note: nm = $10^{-9}$ metres and μm = $10^{-6}$ metres.)

All these optical storage media are used as back-up systems (for photos, music and multimedia files). This also means that CDs and DVDs can be used to transfer files between computers. Manufacturers often supply their software using CDs and DVDs. When the software is supplied in this way, the disk is usually in a read-only format.

The most common use of DVD and Blu-ray is the supply of movies or games. The memory capacity of CDs isn't big enough to store most movies.

## The future of optical media

In recent times both the CD and DVD are showing signs of becoming obsolete. Many computer systems now come with USB connectors only and no DVD or CD drive. The main method of transferring files between devices has become the flash memory. Many people now store all their music in the following ways:

- on hard disk drive systems (set up as sound systems as shown in Figure 6.13)
- in MP3 format on:
  - a computer/tablet
  - their mobile phone
  - a portable music player (such as iPod®)
- using the 'cloud' to store all their files so they can access their music from anywhere in the world
- by 'streaming' their music from the internet; provided the user has an internet connection, they can access music through a laptop computer, mobile phone, tablet or any other receiving device.

It is also a similar story for movies where streaming is becoming increasingly more common. Many television sets are now set up as 'smart' TVs – this means it is now possible to stream movies or television programmes ON DEMAND without the need for any DVD or Blu-ray players. In effect, the television set has become the central computer with a link to the internet using wireless connection.

**Figure 6.13**

Floppy disks met the same fate in the early twenty-first century. How often do you see floppy disks nowadays? It is very likely that CDs and DVDs will meet the same fate and will be replaced by one of the systems described above or something entirely new.

---

## Activity 6.5

Do some research, using this book and the internet, to find out all the different ways to store music files and movie files.

Draw a table and show all the benefits and drawbacks of each of the methods you have identified.

| Storage method | Benefits | Drawbacks |
|---|---|---|
|  |  |  |

---

## USB flash memories

MEMORY STICKS/FLASH MEMORIES (also known as pen drives) use solid-state technology (see Figure 6.14).

They usually connect to a computer through the USB port (see Section 2.2.4).

Their main advantage is that they are very small, lightweight devices which make them suitable as a method for transferring files between computers. They can also be used as small back-up devices for music or photo files, for example.

**Figure 6.14**

Complex or expensive software, such as an Expert System, often uses memory sticks as a DONGLE. The dongle contains additional files which are needed to run the software. Without this dongle, the software won't work properly. It therefore prevents illegal or unauthorised use of the software, and also prevents copying of the software since, without the dongle, it is useless.

Digital cameras (see Section 5.2.4) use a slightly different form of solid-state memory, known as XD (eXtreme Digital) or SD (Secure Digital) cards. The technology is essentially the same as memory sticks. These memory cards allow photos to be transferred from camera to computer via the USB port. Many printers and computers also have card slots allowing the device to read the memory card directly.

Each memory card is made up of NAND chips (see Section 6.4.2) and, as with all solid-state memories, there are no moving parts.

All solid-state memories need to be treated with some care. If they are removed from a device before being made safe (for example, while still in the middle of a read–write operation), data on the memory card or stick can be corrupted. In extreme cases, the memory card or stick become totally unusable. It is essential to wait for the message: 'it is now safe to remove your device' if plugged into a computer. With mobile phones or digital cameras, it is usually advisable to switch them off before removal of the card.

## Removable hard disk drives

REMOVABLE HARD DISK DRIVES are essentially HDD but can be connected to the computer using one of the USB ports. In this way, they can be used as a back-up device or as another way of transferring files between computers.

## 6.5   How to estimate the size of a file

Estimating the size of a text file is relatively straightforward. In Chapter 1 we introduced the idea of ASCII code. Each character from the keyboard has a value of 1 byte.

Suppose we typed in the following message:

This is text from the computer science text book

and then saved it under the filename 'sample_text_for_book'. If we then looked at the properties of the file just saved, we would see:

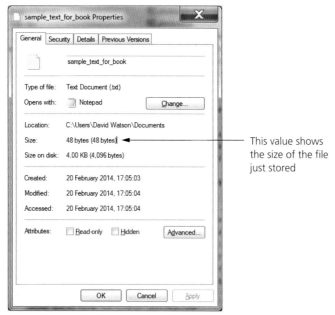

This value shows the size of the file just stored

**Figure 6.15**

If we count the number of characters in the text typed in, we get the number 48. This exactly matches the file size shown in the screenshot in Figure 6.15 – so each character equals 1 byte. We can therefore use this to estimate the size of a text file. Obviously there are other codes stored with the file which make its real size slightly different, but we aren't concerned about that in this section of the book.

Earlier on in the chapter we looked at file sizes for photos and for sound. This is obviously a little more complex, but we saw that one pixel, for example, occupies 3 bytes of memory.

Suppose we imported the photograph shown in Figure 6.16 into a document.

**Figure 6.16**

Looking at the properties of the photograph, we find this:

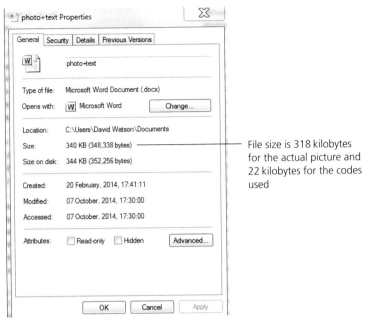

File size is 318 kilobytes for the actual picture and 22 kilobytes for the codes used

**Figure 6.17**

The photograph was 424 by 256 pixels which confirms the file size of 325 632 bytes (318 kilobytes).

## Activity 6.6

a Using Notepad, type in the following message:

> This text should have a file size of over 100 bytes. We can check this by saving the file and then looking at the file properties.

Save your file and then look at its properties and find out the file size of the text you typed in. Was it the value you expected?

b Import a photo into a word processor and check the original file size against the file size of the document. Then import about 3K of text and recheck the file size of the new document. Was the file size as you predicted?

## Activity 6.7

Estimate the size of a file for each of the following:

a Text file containing 256 characters.
b Word processor document containing 1000 characters and a small image which is 256 × 256 pixels in size (assume an extra 14KB for other document features).
c A database is to contain a person's name and their address.
  i Decide the maximum number of characters you would need to input a name and an address.
  ii Estimate the maximum size of file needed to store the name and address.
d A security system contains a password (16 characters long), a username (20 characters long), a small photo (256 × 640 pixels in size) and a security question (up to 72 characters long). Estimate the file size needed to store all this data.

# 7 High- and low-level languages

In this chapter you will learn about:

- programming languages
  - high-level languages
  - low-level languages
- translators
  - compilers
  - interpreters
  - assemblers.

## 7.1 Introduction

People use many different languages to communicate with each other. In order for two people to understand each other they need to speak the same language or another person, an interpreter, is needed to translate from one language to the other language. Programmers use many different programming languages to communicate with computers. Computers only 'understand' their own machine code. A program needs to be translated into machine code before it can be 'understood' by a computer.

## 7.2 Programming languages

### 7.2.1 What is a program?

Programs are our way of telling a computer what to do, how to do it and when to do it. This enables a single computer to perform many different types of task. A computer can be used to stream videos, write reports, provide weather forecasts and many, many other jobs.

An example of a simple task that can be performed by a computer is the provision of a multiplication tables test. Figure 7.1 shows a simple program to set this up and Figure 7.2 shows an example of the test in use.

**Figure 7.2** Program in use

```
when [flag] clicked
set Score to 0
say Multiplication Tables Test for 2 secs
say How many questions can you get right? for 2 secs
repeat 10
  set Number 1 to pick random 2 to 12
  set Number 2 to pick random 2 to 12
  set Result to Number 1 * Number 2
  ask join join Number 1 X Number 2 and wait
  if answer = Result
    change Score by 1
    say You are Right for 2 secs
  else
    say You are Wrong for 2 secs
    say join The Answer was Result for 2 secs
say join Your Total was Score for 2 secs
```

**Figure 7.1** Program written in Scratch

**Activity 7.1**
Find at least **ten** different tasks that computer programs perform in your school.

A COMPUTER PROGRAM is a list of instructions that enable a computer to perform a specific task. Computer programs can be written in high-level languages or low-level languages, depending on the task to be performed and the computer to be used. Most programmers write programs in high-level languages.

## 7.2.2 High-level languages

High-level languages enable a programmer to focus on the problem to be solved and require no knowledge of the hardware and instruction set of the computer that will use the program. Many high-level programming languages are portable and can be used on different types of computer.

High-level languages are designed with programmers in mind; programming statements are easier to understand than those written in a low-level language. This means that programs written in a high-level language are easier to:

- read and understand as the language used is closer to human language
- write in a shorter time
- debug at the development stage
- maintain once in use.

The following snippet of program to add two numbers together is a single program statement written in a typical high-level language. It shows how easy it is to understand what is happening in a high-level language program:

```
Sum := FirstNumber + SecondNumber
```

There are many different high-level programming languages in use today including C++, Delphi, Java, Pascal, Python, Visual Basic and many more. Once a programmer has learnt the techniques of programming in any high-level language, these can be transferred to working in other high-level languages.

**Activity 7.2**
High-level programming languages are said to be problem oriented. What type of problems are the languages named above used for? Find out about **five** more high-level languages. Name each programming language and find out what it is used for.

## 7.2.3 Low-level languages

Low-level languages relate to the specific architecture and hardware of a particular type of computer. Low-level languages can refer to machine code, the binary instructions that a computer understands, or an assembly language that needs to be translated into machine code.

## Assembly languages

Few programmers write programs in an assembly language. Those programmers who do, do so for the following reasons:

- to make use of special hardware
- to make use of special machine-dependent instructions
- to write code that doesn't take up much space in primary memory
- to write code that performs a task very quickly.

The following snippet of program to add two numbers together is written in a typical assembly language and consists of three statements:

```
LDA    First
ADD    Second
STO    Sum
```

In order to understand this program the programmer needs to know that

- LDA means load the value of the variable into the accumulator
- ADD means add the value of another variable to the value stored in the accumulator
- STO means replace the value of the variable by the value stored in the accumulator.

## Activity 7.3

Find out about **two** assembly languages. Name each assembly language and find out what type of computer it is used for.

## Machine code

Programmers do not usually write in machine code as it is difficult to understand and it can be complicated to manage data manipulation and storage.

The following snippet of program to add two numbers together is written in typical machine code, shown in both hexadecimal and binary, and consists of three statements:

| 1 | 12 | 0001 | 00010010 |
|---|----|------|----------|
| 4 | 13 | 0100 | 00010011 |
| 0 | 1A | 0000 | 00011010 |
| **Hexadecimal** | | **Binary** | |

**Figure 7.3**

As you can see, this is not easy to understand in binary! Machine code is usually shown in hexadecimal (see Section 1.5).

## Activity 7.4

Find out about **two** different types of machine code. Name each chip set the machine code is used for and find the codes for load, add and store.

## 7.3  Translators ⊙

Computer programs can exist in several forms.

Programs are written by humans in a form that people who are trained as computer programmers can understand. In order to be used by a computer, programs need to be translated into the binary instructions, or machine code, that the computer understands. Humans find it very difficult to read binary (hexadecimal is easier to understand) and computers can only perform operations written in binary.

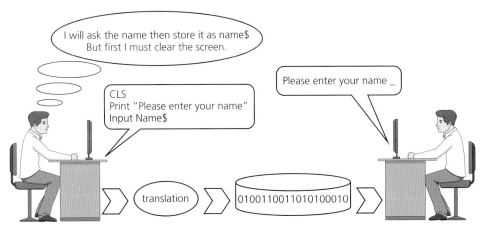

**Figure 7.4** Translation

A program must be translated into binary before a computer can use it; this is done by a utility program called a translator. There are several types of translator program in use; each one performs a different task.

## Compilers

A **COMPILER** is a computer program that translates a program written in a high-level language (HLL) into machine code so that it can be directly used by a computer to perform a required task. Once a program is compiled the machine code can be used again and again to perform the same task without recompilation.

The high-level program statement

```
Sum := FirstNumber + SecondNumber
```

becomes the following machine code instructions when translated

```
0001    00010010
0100    00010011
0000    00011010
```

## Interpreters

An **INTERPRETER** is a computer program that reads a statement from a program written in a high-level language, performs the action specified and then does the same with the next statement and so on.

## Assemblers

An **ASSEMBLER** is a computer program that translates a program written in an assembly language into machine code so that it can be directly used by a computer to perform a required task. Once a program is assembled the machine code can be used again and again to perform the same task without re-assembly.

The assembly language program statements

```
LDA    First
ADD    Second
STO    Sum
```

become the following machine code instructions when translated

```
0001    00010010
0100    00010011
0000    00011010
```

**Table 7.1** Summary of translation programs

| Compiler | Interpreter | Assembler |
|---|---|---|
| Translates a high-level language program into machine code. | Executes a high-level language program a statement at a time. | Translates a low-level language program into machine code. |
| An executable file of machine code is produced. | No executable file of machine code is produced. | An executable file of machine code is produced. |
| One high-level language statement can be translated into several machine code instructions. | One high-level language program statement may require several machine code instructions to be executed. | One low-level language statement is usually translated into one machine code instruction. |
| Compiled programs are used without the compiler. | Interpreted programs cannot be used without the interpreter. | Assembled programs can be used without the assembler. |
| A compiled program is usually distributed for general use. | An interpreter is often used when a program is being developed. | An assembled program is usually distributed for general use. |

## 7.4   What happens when things go wrong?

As programs are written by humans, they may contain errors. There are several different types of error. A SYNTAX ERROR is where a program statement doesn't obey the rules of the programming language. A program cannot be translated if it contains syntax errors. A LOGIC ERROR is where the program doesn't do what the programmer wanted it to do. Logic errors are found when a program is being run.

## 7.4.1 Syntax errors

When a program is being compiled, if any syntax errors are found no translated program is produced. Instead, a list of all the errors in the whole program is produced. The programmer corrects these errors and recompiles the program.

When a program is being interpreted, the interpreter performs the actions specified by each statement until a syntax error is found. The programmer is then alerted to the place in the program where the error was found. The error is corrected by the programmer and the interpretation continues until the next error is found or the task is completed.

## 7.4.2 Logic errors

When a program is being run, if it doesn't do what it should do there is a logic error. These can be found by tracing what the program does and using test data with expected results – see Chapter 9.

### 7.4.3 Using an Integrated/Interactive Development Environment (IDE)

Most high-level programming languages offer the use of an IDE for program development. This contains an editor with an interpreter and/or compiler together with debugging tools, which can improve the speed of program development.

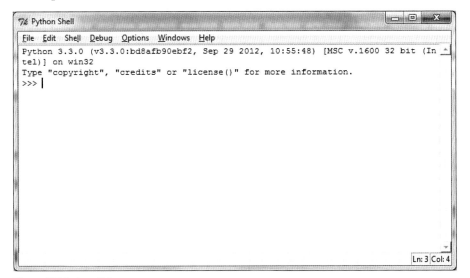

**Figure 7.5** Python IDE

### Activity 7.5

Have a look at the development environment you are using for programming – is it an IDE? What facilities are offered to help with program development?

## End-of-chapter questions

1 Use the words below to complete the following sentences.

   assembler     compiler     interpreter

To translate a program written in a high-level language, you can use a _____ or an _____. To translate a program written in a low-level language you must use an _____.

2
**Table 7.2**

| Program A | Program B |
|---|---|
| BEGIN | INP |
| VAR First, Second: INTEGER | STA FIRST |
| READ First, Second | INP |
| First:= First + Second | STA SECOND |
| WRITE First | LDA FIRST |
| END | ADD SECOND |
| | STA FIRST |
| | OUT |
| | FIRST DAT |
| | SECOND DAT |

   a  Which program is easier to understand?
   b  Why is it easier to understand?
   c  Which program is written in a high-level language?

3 Give **three** advantages of writing a program in a high-level language rather than using a low-level language.

4 Give **three** advantages of writing a program in a low-level language rather than using a high-level language.

5 Explain what a **compiler** does and what an **interpreter** does. In your explanation include a description of the differences between them.

6 Choose which type of translator you would use to develop a program written in a high-level programming language. Give **three** reasons to support your choice.

7 Look at these two pieces of code:

```
A   CLC
    LDX #0
Loop: LDA A, X
        ABC B, X
        STA C, X
        INX
        CPX #16
        BNE loop
```

```
B   FOR loop = 1 TO 4
    INPUT Number1, Number2
    Sum = Number1 + Number2
    Print Sum
    NEXT
```

   a  Which of these pieces of code is written in a high-level language?  [1]
   b  Give **one** benefit of writing code in a high-level language.  [1]
   c  Give **one** benefit of writing code in a low-level language.  [1]
   d  High-level languages can be *compiled* or *interpreted*.
      Give **two** differences between a compiler and an interpreter.  [2]

*Cambridge IGCSE Computer Studies 7010/0420*
*Paper 12 Q13 June 2012*

# 8 Security and ethics

In this chapter you will learn about:

- keeping data safe from accidental or malicious damage
- keeping data safe from unauthorised users
- use of passwords, firewalls, proxy servers, SSL, TLS and encryption
- risks posed by phishing and pharming
- security safeguards when carrying out online transactions
- computer ethics.

## 8.1 Introduction

Keeping data safe is extremely important for a number of reasons. It may be personal data that you want to keep within your family or your close friends, or commercial data, such as passwords and bank account details, which need to be kept safe to protect your money.

Data can be corrupted or deleted either through accidental damage or through a malicious act. There are many ways to keep data safe and some of the methods available will be covered in this chapter.

There is also a short section on computer ethics since this is becoming an increasingly important topic for discussion.

## 8.2 Security and data integrity

Whether a user is working on an off-line computer or on a computer connected to the internet, keeping data safe is very important.

Data is threatened by malicious software, hackers or accidental damage. This section covers a number of different security risks and considers ways to overcome or minimise them.

Each security risk, together with its description, possible effects and risk mitigation will be set out as follows:

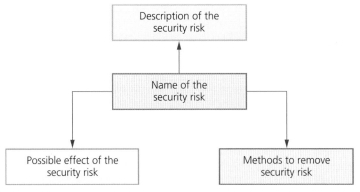

Figure 8.1

## 8.2.1 Hacking

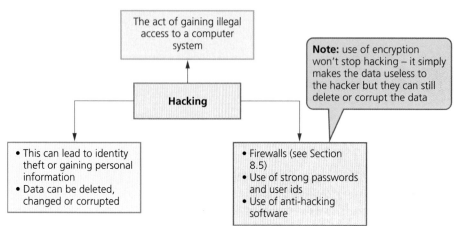

**Figure 8.2**

Note the difference between CRACKING and HACKING.

Hacking is breaking into a computer system to steal personal data without the owner's consent or knowledge (e.g. to steal a password file).

Cracking is where someone edits a program source code (i.e. looks for a 'back door' in the software so that the code can be exploited or changed for a specific purpose). This is usually done for a malicious purpose (e.g. legitimate software could be altered by a cracker to perform a different task e.g. send a user to a specific website).

Essentially, hacking isn't necessarily harmful whilst cracking is ALWAYS totally illegal and is potentially very damaging.

## 8.2.2 Viruses

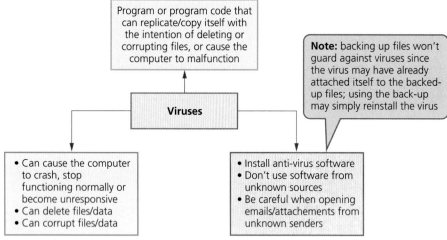

**Figure 8.3**

# 8.2.3 Phishing

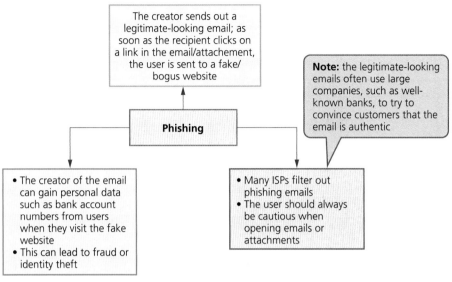

**Figure 8.4**

# 8.2.4 Pharming

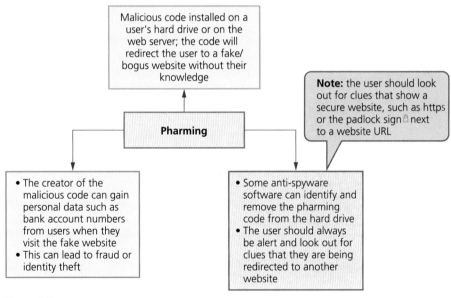

**Figure 8.5**

## 8.2.5 Wardriving

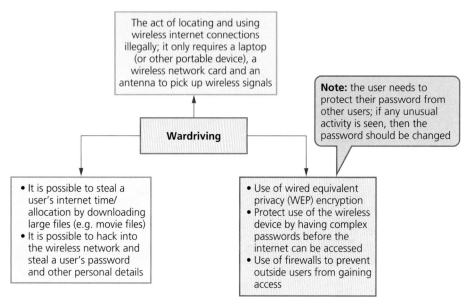

**Figure 8.6**

## 8.2.6 Spyware/key-logging software

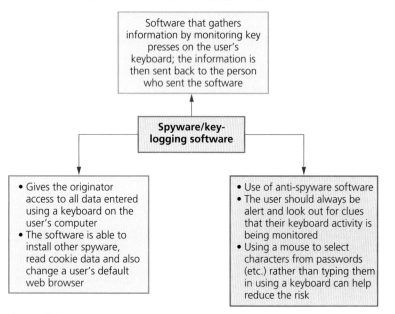

**Figure 8.7**

## 8.3   Cookies

A cookie is a packet of information sent by a web server to a web browser. Cookies are generated each time the user visits the website. A message is frequently displayed saying 'cookies are required to access this site' (or some equivalent message). Every time a user visits the website, cookies will have collected some key information about the user. They are able to carry out user tracking and also maintain user preferences (for example, when a user buys a CD on a music website, the cookies will have remembered the user's previous buying habits and a message like this often follows: 'Customers who bought items in your Recent History also bought: YYYY').

Cookies aren't programs but are simply pieces of data. They can't actually perform any operations. They only allow the detection of web pages viewed by a user on a particular website and store user preferences, as described above.

The information gathered by cookies forms an ANONYMOUS USER PROFILE and doesn't contain personal information (such as credit card numbers or passwords). Because of the information they do collect, however, they are subject to privacy and security concerns.

## 8.4  Loss of data and data corruption

Section 8.2 considered a number of security issues which could lead to loss of data or the corruption of data.

This section covers the potential impact on data caused by:

- accidental mal-operation
- hardware malfunction
- software malfunction

on a computer system. In each case:

- safeguards
- recovery methods

to prevent the loss or corruption of data are considered.

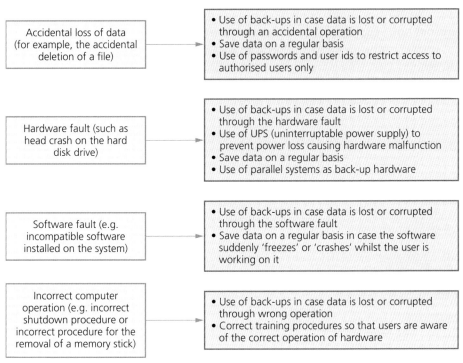

**Figure 8.8**

## 8.5   Firewalls and proxy servers

A FIREWALL can be either software or hardware. It sits between the user's computer and an external network (e.g. the internet) and filters information in and out of the computer.

**Figure 8.9**

Tasks carried out by a firewall include:

- examining the 'traffic' between the user's computer (or internal network) and a public network (e.g. the internet)
- checking whether incoming or outgoing data meets a given set of criteria
- if the data fails the criteria, the firewall will block the 'traffic' and give the user (or network manager) a warning that there may be a security issue
- logging all incoming and outgoing 'traffic' to allow later interrogation by the user (or network manager)
- criteria can be set to prevent access to certain undesirable sites; the firewall can keep a list of all undesirable IP addresses
- helping to prevent viruses or hackers entering the user's computer (or internal network)
- warning the user if some software on their system is trying to access an external data source (e.g. automatic software upgrade); the user is given the option of allowing it to go ahead or requesting that such access is denied.

The firewall can be a hardware interface which is located somewhere between the computer (or internal network external link) and the internet connection. It is often referred to in this case as a GATEWAY. Alternatively, the firewall can be software installed on a computer; in some cases, this is part of the operating system.

However, there are certain circumstances where the firewall can't prevent potential harmful 'traffic':

- it cannot prevent individuals, on internal networks, using their own modems to bypass the firewall
- employee misconduct or carelessness cannot be controlled by firewalls (for example, control of passwords or use of accounts)
- users on stand-alone computers can chose to disable the firewall, leaving their computer open to harmful 'traffic' from the internet.

All of these issues require management control or personal control (on a single computer) to ensure that the firewall is allowed to do its job effectively.

PROXY SERVERS act as an intermediary between the user and a web server:

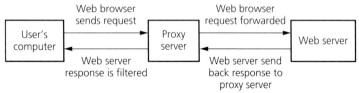

**Figure 8.10**

Functions of proxy servers include:

- allowing the internet 'traffic' to be filtered; they can block access to a website if necessary (similar type or reaction as a firewall)
- by using the feature known as a CACHE, they can speed up access to information from a website; when the website is first visited, the home page is stored on the proxy server; when the user next visits the website, it now goes through the proxy server cache instead, giving much faster access
- keeping the user's IP address secret – this clearly improves security
- acting as a firewall.

## 8.6   Security protocols

We will now consider two forms of security protocols when using the internet:

- Secure Sockets Layer (SSL)
- Transport Layer Security (TLS).

SECURE SOCKETS LAYER (SSL) is a type of protocol (a set of rules used by computers to communicate with each other across a network). This allows data to be sent and received securely over the internet.

When a user logs onto a website, SSL encrypts the data – only the user's computer and the web server are able to make sense of what is being transmitted. A user will know if SSL is being applied when they see https or the small padlock in the status bar at the top of the screen. So what happens when a user wants to access a secure website and receive and send data to it?

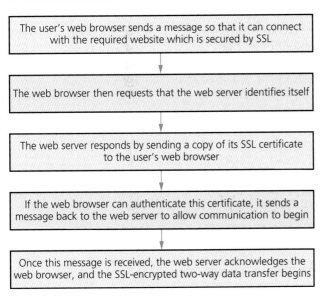

**Figure 8.11**

TRANSPORT LAYER SECURITY (TLS) is similar to SSL but is a more recent security system. TLS is a form of protocol that ensures the security and privacy of data between devices and users when communicating over the internet. It is essentially designed to provide encryption, authentication and data integrity in a more effective way than its predecessor SSL.

When a website and client (user) communicate over the internet, TLS is designed to prevent a third party hacking into this communication causing problems with data security.

TLS is formed of two layers:

- record protocol: this part of the communication can be used with or without encryption (it contains the data being transferred over the internet).
- handshake protocol: this permits the website and the client (user) to authenticate each other and to make use of encryption algorithms (a secure session between client and website is established).

Only the most recent web browsers support both SSL and TLS which is why the older SSL is still used in many cases. But what are the main differences between SSL and TLS since they both effectively do the same thing?

- It is possible to extend TLS by adding new authentication methods.
- TLS can make use of SESSION CACHING which improves the overall performance compared to SSL (see Section 8.6.1).
- TLS separates the handshaking process from the record protocol (layer) which holds all the data.

## 8.6.1 Session caching

When opening a TLS session, it requires a lot of computer time (due mainly to the complex encryption keys being used – see Section 8.7). The use of session caching can avoid the need to utilise so much computer time for each connection. TLS can either establish a new session or attempt to resume an existing session; using the latter can considerably boost system performance.

## 8.7  Encryption

Encryption is used primarily to protect data in case it has been hacked. Whilst encryption won't prevent hacking, it makes the data meaningless unless the recipient has the necessary decryption tools described below.

There are two types of encryption:

- symmetric
- asymmetric or public key.

## 8.7.1 Symmetric encryption

SYMMETRIC ENCRYPTION is a secret key which can be a combination of characters. If this key is applied to a message, its content is changed which makes it unreadable unless the recipient also has the decryption key.

One key is needed to encrypt a message and another key is needed to decrypt a message.

It is obviously important that the sender and receiver have the same encryption and decryption key. There is clearly a security risk here, since the sender has to supply the key to the recipient. This key could be intercepted by, for example, a hacker which puts the security of the encrypted message at risk. This situation is referred to as the KEY DISTRIBUTION PROBLEM.

So the question is, how can both sender and receiver have the required key without sending it electronically in some way? The following routine shows how this is done. Follow it through, and you will see that both sender and recipient end up with a key which is effectively secret, but didn't involve sending the actual key electronically.

**Table 8.1**

| Stage | Sender | Recipient |
|---|---|---|
| 1 | The sender uses an encryption algorithm (see Section 8.7.3) and chooses a value<br><br>e.g. X = 2 (this is kept secret) | The recipient uses the same algorithm and also chooses a value<br><br>e.g. Y = 4 (this is also kept secret) |
| 2 | This value of X is put into a simple algorithm:<br><br>$7^X$ (MOD 11)<br><br>(MOD gives the remainder when dividing a number by 11)<br><br>This gives:<br><br>$7^2$ (MOD 11) = 49 (MOD 11)<br><br>which gives the value:<br><br>5 (i.e. 4 remainder 5) | The value of Y is put into the same algorithm:<br><br>$7^Y$ (MOD 11)<br><br>(MOD gives the remainder when dividing a number by 11)<br><br>This gives:<br><br>$7^4$ (MOD 11) = 2401 (MOD 11)<br><br>which gives the value:<br><br>3 (i.e. 218 remainder 3) |
| 3 | The sender now sends the value just calculated (i.e. 5) to the recipient | The recipient now sends the value just calculated (i.e. 3) to the sender |
| 4 | This new value is put into the same algorithm – the new value replaces '7':<br><br>$3^X$ (MOD 11)<br><br>This gives:<br><br>$3^2$ (MOD 11) = 9 (MOD 11)<br><br>which gives the value:<br><br>9 (i.e. 0 remainder 9) | This new value is put into the same algorithm – the new value replaces '7':<br><br>$5^Y$ (MOD 11)<br><br>This gives:<br><br>$5^4$ (MOD 11) = 625 (MOD 11)<br><br>which gives the value:<br><br>9 (i.e. 56 remainder 9) |

Thus both sender and recipient end up with the same encryption and decryption key of 9. This gives us the basis of how an encryption key can be generated.

## Activity 8.1

Use the following sender and receiver values to check that the system described in Table 8.1 works:

a sender uses the value x = 3 and receiver uses the value y = 5

b sender uses the value x = 7 and receiver uses the value y = 6

Table 8.1 refers to an ENCRYPTION ALGORITHM. As we will see in Section 8.7.3, messages are put through an encryption algorithm to produce a message in encrypted form. This algorithm uses an encryption key to produce a message which appears meaningless unless the same key is applied to 'unlock' the original message. The key is referred to as an encryption key or a decryption key depending whether it is used to encrypt the message or to decrypt the message.

The next section discusses the types of encryption keys.

## 8.7.2 Asymmetric encryption

The risks surrounding symmetric encryption keys have already been discussed. A more secure method is to use ASYMMETRIC or PUBLIC KEY encryption. A PRIVATE KEY and a public key are both needed:

- public key is made available to everybody
- private key is only known by the computer user.

Both types of key are needed to encrypt and decrypt messages. Imagine a user on computer A wants to send a private message to a user on computer B; how is asymmetric encryption used?

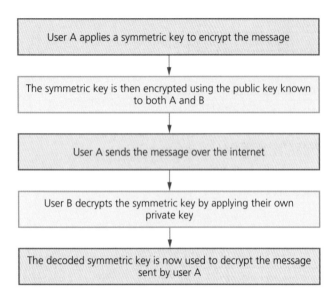

**Figure 8.12**

The encryption keys are often generated by using a HASHING ALGORITHM. This is actually very different to an encryption algorithm. The hashing algorithm takes a message or a key and translates it into a string of characters usually shown in hex notation (the length of the string depends on the algorithm being used). This essentially makes the message or key almost impossible to read if it is somehow intercepted by, for example, a hacker. The same hashing algorithm has to be applied at both ends (sender and receiver) for the message or key to be understood.

In summary, the encryption algorithm converts messages using an encryption key into 'meaningless' text; the same key has to be used to decrypt the message. These keys can, however, be intercepted which makes the encryption process less secure. To overcome this problem, a hashing algorithm is applied to the message or key, producing a string of characters which are virtually impossible to 'break' if intercepted. This considerably increases the security of the whole process when sending personal or sensitive data across, for example, the internet. The use of hashing and encryption is further discussed in Section 8.7.4.

An example of a well-known hashing algorithm is MD4 which generates a 128-bit string whenever a value is run through it. For example, the following 16-digit code:

**1234 5678 9012 3456**

would produce the following value when put through the MD4 hashing algorithm:

**543FC7DDEA0CF5EAF84279CBADCA180D**

(Note: this contains 32 hexadecimal digits (i.e. 128 bits) – see Section 1.5.)

Strings which are 128 bits long give $3 \times 10^{38}$ possible combinations which makes them very secure. Some newer systems use 256-bit strings which have $1 \times 10^{77}$ possible combinations. Older systems employ strings which are only 56 bits in length, which gives them only $7 \times 10^{16}$ possibilities – this has become relatively easy to break since modern computers are so fast at number crunching!

But it is clear that the larger the key size, the more secure the encryption will be.

## 8.7.3 Plain text and cypher text

PLAIN TEXT (sometimes written as a single word 'plaintext') is described as the text or normal representation of data before it goes through an encryption algorithm.

CYPHER TEXT (sometimes written as 'cyphertext' or 'ciphertext') is the output from an encryption algorithm:

**Figure 8.13**

## 8.7.4 Authentication

AUTHENTICATION is used to verify that data comes from a trusted source. It works *with* encryption to strengthen internet security.

Examples include:

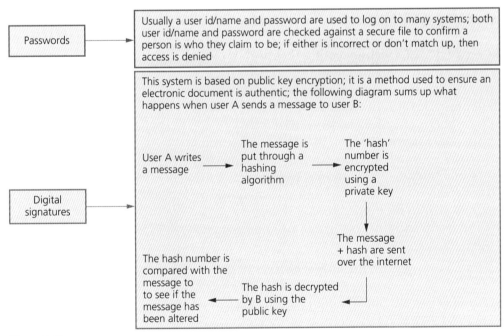

**Figure 8.14**

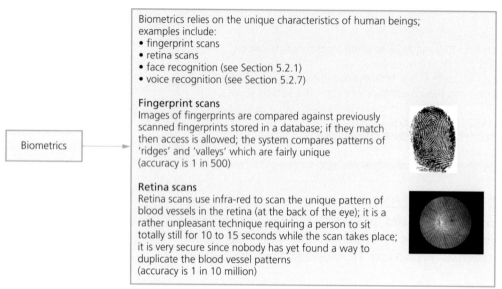

Biometrics relies on the unique characteristics of human beings; examples include:
• fingerprint scans
• retina scans
• face recognition (see Section 5.2.1)
• voice recognition (see Section 5.2.7)

**Fingerprint scans**
Images of fingerprints are compared against previously scanned fingerprints stored in a database; if they match then access is allowed; the system compares patterns of 'ridges' and 'valleys' which are fairly unique
(accuracy is 1 in 500)

**Retina scans**
Retina scans use infra-red to scan the unique pattern of blood vessels in the retina (at the back of the eye); it is a rather unpleasant technique requiring a person to sit totally still for 10 to 15 seconds while the scan takes place; it is very secure since nobody has yet found a way to duplicate the blood vessel patterns
(accuracy is 1 in 10 million)

Biometrics

**Figure 8.14** continued

## 8.7.5 Denial of service attacks

**A denial of service attack** (DoS) is an attempt at preventing users from accessing part of a network, notably an internet server. This is usually temporary but may be a very damaging act or a big breach of security. It doesn't just affect networks; an individual can also be a target for such an attack.

The attacker may be able to prevent a user from:

● accessing their emails
● accessing websites/web pages
● accessing online services (such as banking).

One method of attack is to flood the network with useless traffic. How does this cause the problem?

When a user types in or clicks on a URL of a website (using their web browser), a request is sent to the internet server which contains the website or web page. Obviously, the server can only handle a finite number of requests. So if it becomes overloaded by an attacker sending out thousands of requests, it won't be able to service the user's legitimate request. This is effectively a denial of service.

This can happen to a user's email account, for example, by an attacker sending out many spam messages to their email account. Internet Service Providers (ISPs) only allow a specific data quota for each user. Consequently, if the attacker sends out very large or many hundreds of emails to the user's account, it will quickly get clogged up and the user won't be able to receive legitimate emails.

An individual user or a website can guard against these attacks to some degree by:

● using an up-to-date malware/virus checker
● setting up a firewall to restrict traffic to and from the internet server or user's computer
● applying email filters to manage or filter out unwanted traffic or spam emails.

Signs that a user can look out for to see if they are a victim of one of these attacks include:

● slow network performance (opening files or accessing certain websites)
● unavailability or inability to access particular websites
● large amounts of spam mail reaching the user's email account.

## 8.8  Applications

Online banking and shopping are all at risk from many of the security issues described earlier on.

We will now consider some of the ways banks protect their customers from online fraud. The following notes are in addition to safeguards such as encryption, SSL, virus scanners and many of the other ways described in the earlier part of this chapter and refer to additional features you might see as part of a bank's security system.

When a customer logs on to a banking website and carries out a transaction, encryption is used to protect the customer's personal details. However, banks carry out a number of other procedures to give additional protection. Not all of the methods described would be used by one bank. However, the notes give some idea of the type of safeguards that might be encountered when a customer logs on to a bank's website.

1  Many banks use a 10- or 12-digit code unique to the customer:

**HODDER BANK**

Please enter your unique 12-digit code:

**Figure 8.15**

2  You may then be asked to input three random numbers from a four-digit PIN and/or three characters from a 10-character password (this will vary from bank to bank, of course):

**HODDER BANK**

Please enter the following digits from your PIN:

1$^{st}$ digit
4$^{th}$ digit
3$^{rd}$ digit

Please enter the following characters from your password:

2$^{nd}$
4$^{th}$
9$^{th}$

**Figure 8.16**

3  Some systems use a hand-held device into which the customer inserts their card. They will be asked to enter their PIN. The device will then generate an eight-digit code which the customer types into the web page of the bank. This eight-digit code is generated from an internal clock and PIN. The bank's server and the time are both synchronised with the hand-held device; the server also stores the PIN. The bank's server will therefore know if the eight-digit code entered is correct. Each eight-digit code is only valid for a few minutes before it has to be redone.

This system defeats hackers and spyware since the code will change every time the customer logs on to the bank's website.

**Figure 8.17**

4 Some banking systems ask the customer to key in parts of their password using drop-down boxes. This is an attempt to defeat spyware/key-logging software. Each of the requested characters from the password are entered by selecting a character from a drop-down menu using a mouse, thus eliminating the use of a keyboard.

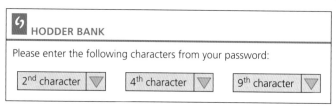

**Figure 8.18**

5 Once all these stages have been passed, some systems then ask for personal data, such as:
- 'You last logged into the system on 15th September 2015. Is that correct?'
- 'Your mobile phone number is: 9777 111 2222. Is that correct?'
- 'What is your mother's maiden name?'

6 Assuming the customer successfully negotiates all of the security 'hurdles', they will be sent to a home page on the website. Once you are there, it is important to only use the bank's navigation tools rather than the ones at the top of the screen. Otherwise you will be logged out of the system, and you will need to go through all the earlier steps again.

## 8.9  Computer ethics

COMPUTER ETHICS is a set of principles set out to regulate the use of computers. Three factors are considered:

- INTELLECTUAL PROPERTY RIGHTS – this covers, for example, copying of software without the permission of the owner
- PRIVACY ISSUES – this covers, for example, hacking or any illegal access to another person's personal data
- effect of computers on society – this covers factors such as job losses, social impacts and so on.

Use of the internet has led to an increase in *plagiarism* – this is when a person takes another person's idea/work and claims it as their own. Whilst it is perfectly fine to quote another person's idea, it is essential that some acknowledgement is made so that the originator of the idea is known to others. This can be done by a series of references at the end of a document or footnotes on each page where a reference needs to be made. Software exists that can scan text and then look for examples of plagiarism by searching web pages on the internet.

The ACM (Association for Computer Machinery) and IEEE (Institute of Electrical and Electronics Engineers) have published the following code of ethics:

1. to accept responsibility in making decisions consistent with the safety, health and welfare of the public, and to disclose promptly the factors that might endanger the public or the environment;

2. to avoid real or perceived conflicts of interest whenever possible, and to disclose them to affected parties when they do exist;

3. to be honest and realistic in stating claims or estimates based on available data;

4. to reject bribery in all its forms;

5. to improve the understanding of technology; its appropriate application, and potential consequences;

6. to maintain and improve our technical competence and to undertake technological tasks for others only if qualified by training or experience, or after full disclosure of pertinent limitations;

7. to seek, accept, and offer honest criticism of technical work, to acknowledge and correct errors, and to credit properly the contributions of others;

8. to treat fairly all persons and to not engage in acts of discrimination based on race, religion, gender, disability, age, national origin, sexual orientation, gender identity, or gender expression;

9. to avoid injuring others, their property, reputation, or employment by false or malicious action;

10. to assist colleagues and co-workers in their professional development and to support them in following this code of ethics.

*Reproduced with kind permission of the IEEEE*

## 8.10 Free software, freeware and shareware

Apart from the usual commercial software (such as spreadsheets and word processors) which are all sold in shops for a profit, there is a group of software which causes much confusion among many users. This group consists of:

- free software
- freeware
- shareware.

The final part of this chapter will explain the fundamental differences between these types of software.

## 8.10.1 Free software

Users have the freedom to run, copy, change or adapt free software. Examples include: F-spot (photograph manager), Scribus (DTP) and Abiword (word processor).

The originators of this type of software stress this is based on *liberty* and not *price*. This means that a user is guaranteed the freedom to study and modify the software source code in any way to suit their requirements.

Essentially a user is allowed to do the following:

- run the software for any legal purpose they wish
- study the source code and modify it as necessary to meet their needs
- pass the software (in either original or modified form) on to friends, family or colleagues.

A user of the software doesn't need to seek permission to do any of the above actions since it isn't protected by any copyright restrictions. However, it is important to realise that there are certain rules that need to be obeyed. The user

- cannot add source code from another piece of software unless this is also described as free software
- cannot produce software which copies existing software subject to copyright laws
- cannot adapt the software in such a way that it infringes copyright laws protecting other software
- may not use the source code to produce software which is deemed offensive by third parties.

## 8.10.2 Freeware

FREEWARE is software a user can download from the internet free of charge. Once it has been downloaded, there are no fees associated with using the software (examples include: Adobe, Skype or media players).

Unlike free software, freeware is subject to copyright laws and users are often requested to tick a box to say they understand and agree to the terms and conditions governing the software. This basically means that a user is not allowed to study or modify the source code in any way.

## 8.10.3 Shareware

In this case, users are allowed to try out some software free of charge for a trial period. At the end of the trial period, the author of the software will request that you pay a fee if you like it. Once the fee is paid, a user is registered with the originator of the software and free updates and help are then provided. Very often, the trial version of the software is missing some of the features found in the full version, and these don't become available until the fee is paid.

Obviously, this type of software is fully protected by copyright laws and a user must make sure they don't use the source code in any of their own software. Permission needs to be obtained before this software is copied and given to friends, family or colleagues.

## Activity 8.3

A software company offers a suite of shareware programs (containing a spreadsheet, word processor, database and drawing package).
What are the benefits to:

- the company
- the customer

of offering software packages as shareware?

(Note: ethical issues are raised as electronic communication continues to grow. Earlier in this chapter, issues such as hacking, viruses and other malware were considered. All of these put users at risk when using the internet or indeed any electronic device which transmits and receives data over a live link (e.g. mobile phones, tablets and other devices).

Many users are aware that computers can undergo hacking or virus attack (and any of the other security issues outlined earlier) but don't seem to be aware that devices such as mobile phones are also vulnerable to attack by hackers and other people intent on causing harm to users of electronic devices.)

**Chapters**

# 9 Problem-solving and design

## 9.1 Introduction

In order to build a computer system that performs a specific task or solves a given problem, the task or problem has to be clearly defined, showing what is going to be computed and how it is going to be computed. This chapter introduces the tools and techniques that are used to design a software solution that together with the associated computer hardware will form a computer system.

## 9.1.1 What is a computer system?

A COMPUTER SYSTEM is made up of software, data, hardware, communications and people; each computer system can be divided up into a set of sub-systems. Each sub-system can be further divided into sub-systems and so on until each sub-system just performs a single action.

Computer systems can be very large or very small or any size in between; most people interact with many different computer systems during their daily life without realising it. For example, when I wake up in the morning I use an app on my smart phone for my alarm, I then check the weather forecast on my computer before I drive to work. The alarm program is a very small computer system; when I check the weather forecast I obtain information from one of the largest computer systems in the world.

> **Activity 9.1**
> Identify at least **five** computer systems you frequently use in your daily life. See if you can decide the size of each system.

## 9.1.2 Tools and techniques

In order to understand how a computer system is built up and how it works, it is often divided up into sub-systems. This division can be shown using top-down design to produce structure diagrams that demonstrate the modular construction of the system. Each sub-system can be developed by a programmer as sub-routine or an existing library routine may be already available for use. How each sub-routine works can be shown by using flowcharts or pseudocode.

## Top-down design

TOP-DOWN DESIGN is the breaking down of a computer system into a set of sub-systems, then breaking each sub-system down into a set of smaller sub-systems, until each sub-system just performs a single action. This is an effective way of designing a computer system to provide a solution to a problem, since each part of the problem is broken down into smaller more manageable problems. The process of breaking down into smaller sub-systems is called 'stepwise refinement'.

This structured approach works for the development of both large and small computer systems. When large computer systems are being developed this means that several programmers can work independently to develop and test different sub-systems for the same system at the same time. This reduces the development and testing time.

## Structure diagrams

In order to show top-down design in a diagrammatic form, structure diagrams can be used. The STRUCTURE DIAGRAM shows the design of a computer system in a hierarchical way, with each level giving a more detailed breakdown of the system into sub-systems.

## Alarm app for a smart phone

Consider the alarm app computer system for a smart phone. This could be divided into three sub-systems, setting the alarm, checking for the alarm time, sounding the alarm. These sub-systems could then be further sub-divided; the structure diagram makes the process clearer.

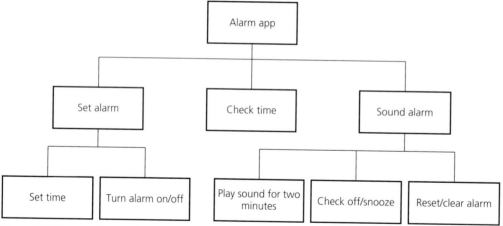

**Figure 9.1** Structure diagram for alarm app

### Activity 9.2
Break down the 'check time' sub-system from the smart phone alarm app into further sub-systems.

### Activity 9.3
Draw a structure diagram for cleaning your teeth.

# Flowcharts

A **FLOWCHART** shows diagrammatically the steps required for a task (sub-system) and the order that they are to be performed. These steps together with the order are called an **ALGORITHM**. Flowcharts are an effective way to communicate the algorithm that shows how a system or sub-system works. How to construct flowcharts is covered in Chapter 10.

Have a look at a flowchart for the checking-for-the-alarm-time sub-system.

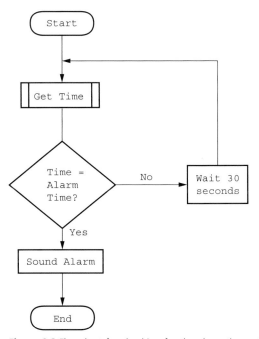

**Figure 9.2** Flowchart for checking-for-the-alarm-time sub-system

# Pseudocode

**PSEUDOCODE** is a simple method of showing an algorithm, using English-like words and mathematical operators that are set out to look like a program. How to write algorithms in pseudocode is covered in Chapter 10.

Have a look at the pseudocode for the checking-for-the-alarm-time algorithm.

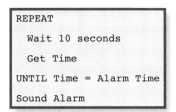

**Figure 9.3** Pseudocode for the checking-for-the-alarm-time algorithm

# Library routines

A **LIBRARY ROUTINE** is a set of programming instructions for a given task that is already available for use. It is pre-tested and usually performs a task that is frequently required. For example, the task 'get time' in the checking-for-the-alarm-time algorithm would probably be readily available as a library routine.

## Sub-routines

A SUB-ROUTINE is a set of programming instructions for a given task that forms a sub-system, not the whole system. Sub-routines written in high-level programming languages are called 'procedures' or 'functions' depending on how they are used. See Chapter 11 for further details.

## 9.2 Algorithms

An ALGORITHM sets out the steps to complete a given task. This is usually shown as a flowchart or pseudocode. Anyone who studies the flowchart or algorithm should be able to work out the purpose of the task.

### Activity 9.4

Have a look at the flowchart and pseudocode below. What is the purpose of the algorithm that they both represent?
What would be output if the numbers 7 and 18 were input?

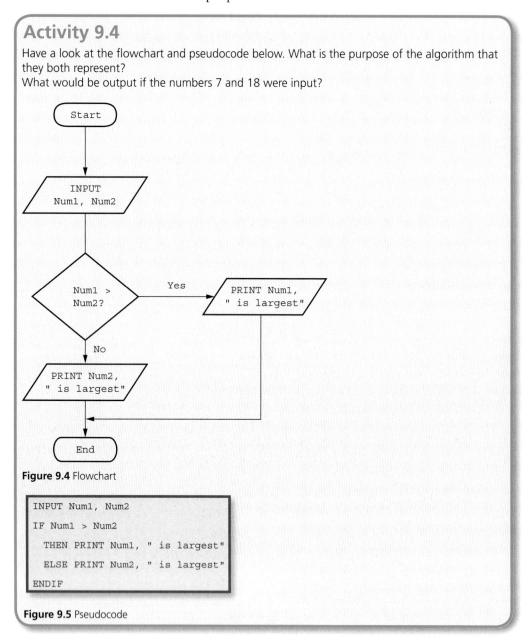

**Figure 9.4** Flowchart

```
INPUT Num1, Num2
IF Num1 > Num2
  THEN PRINT Num1, " is largest"
  ELSE PRINT Num2, " is largest"
ENDIF
```

**Figure 9.5** Pseudocode

For more complicated tasks just inspecting the flowchart or pseudocode may not be an accurate way of determining its purpose; a more structured thorough approach is required. This will require the use of test data and trace tables.

Some tasks are required frequently and there are standard methods of completing them, for example, taking the square root of a number or sorting a list of names into alphabetical order. These standard solutions can be provided by a high-level programming language as a standard function or procedure, for example, mathematical functions such as max or min. Library routines are also available for standard methods such as sorting or searching.

## 9.3  Test data

In order to determine whether a solution is working as it should, it needs to be tested. Usually before a whole system is tested each sub-system is tested separately.

Algorithms can be tested by a person working through them using any data that is required and seeing what the result is; computer programs can be tested by running them on a computer using any data that is required and seeing what result is output. In order to test a solution thoroughly it may need to be worked through several times with different sets of test data.

A SET OF TEST DATA is all the items of data required to work through a solution. The set of test data used in the activity above was 7 and 18.

Testing needs to be done to prove that the solution works correctly. In order to do this a set of test data should be used together with the result(s) that are expected from that data. The type of test data used to do this is called NORMAL DATA, this should be used to work through the solution to find the actual result(s) and see if these are the same as the expected result(s).

For example, here is a set of normal test data for an algorithm to record the percentage marks from 10 end-of-term examinations for a student and find their average mark:

Normal test data: 50, 50, 50, 50, 50, 50 50, 50, 50, 50

Expected result: 50

### Activity 9.5
Provide another set of test data and its expected result.

Testing also needs to be done to prove that the solution does not give incorrect results. In order to do this, test data should be used that will be rejected as the values are not suitable. This type of test data is called ERRONEOUS or ABNORMAL TEST DATA; it should be rejected by the solution.

For example erroneous/abnormal data for an algorithm to record the percentage marks from 10 end-of-term examinations for a student and find their average mark could be:

Erroneous/abnormal data: −12, eleven

Expected results: these values should be rejected

### Activity 9.6
Provide some more erroneous/abnormal data for this algorithm and its expected results.

When testing algorithms with numerical values, sometimes only a given range of values should be allowed. For example, percentage marks should only be in the range 0 to 100. The algorithm should be tested with EXTREME DATA, which, in this case, are the largest and smallest marks that should be accepted. Extreme data are the largest and smallest values that normal data can take.

Extreme data: 0, 100

Expected results: these values should be accepted

There is another type of test data called BOUNDARY DATA; this is used to establish where the largest and smallest values occur. For example, for percentage marks in the range 0 to 100, the algorithm should be tested with the following boundary data; at each boundary two values are required, one value is accepted and the other value is rejected.

Boundary data for 0 is −1, 0

Expected results: −1 is rejected, 0 is accepted

## Activity 9.7
Provide boundary data for the upper end of the range; assume that the percentage marks are always whole numbers.

## Activity 9.8
The end-of-term examinations are now marked out of 20. Provide the following:

a two sets of normal data and their expected results
b some erroneous/abnormal data and their expected results
c two sets of boundary data and their expected results.

## 9.4   Validation and verification

In order for computer systems to only accept data inputs that are reasonable and accurate, every item of data needs to be examined before it is accepted by the system. Two different methods, with very similar sounding names, are used. For data entry, VALIDATION is performed automatically by the computer system to ensure that only data is that is reasonable is accepted and VERIFICATION is used to check that the data does not change as it is being entered.

## 9.4.1 Validation

Validation is the automated checking by a program that data is reasonable before it is accepted into a computer system. Different types of check may be used on the same piece of data; for example an examination mark could be checked for reasonableness by using a range check, a type check and a presence check. When data is validated by a computer system, if the data is rejected a message should be output explaining why the data was rejected and another opportunity given to enter the data.

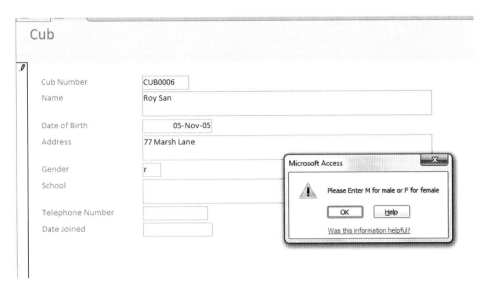

**Figure 9.6** Data entry error message

There are many different types of validation checks including:

- range checks
- length checks
- type checks
- character checks
- format checks
- presence checks
- check digits.

A RANGE CHECK checks that only numbers within a specified range are accepted. For example percentage marks between 0 and 100 inclusive.

A LENGTH CHECK checks either:

- that data contains an exact number of characters, for example that a password must be exactly eight characters in length so that passwords with seven or fewer characters or nine or more characters would be rejected

or

- that the data entered is a reasonable number of characters, for example a family name could be between two and 30 characters inclusive so that names with one character or 31 or more characters would be rejected.

A TYPE CHECK checks that the data entered is of a given data type, for example number of brothers or sisters would be an integer (whole number).

A CHARACTER CHECK checks that when a string of characters is entered it does not contain any invalid characters or symbols, for example a name would not contain characters such as %, and a telephone number would only contain digits or (, ), and +.

A FORMAT CHECK checks that the characters entered conform to a pre-defined pattern, for example in Figure 9.6 the cub number must be in the form CUB9999.

A PRESENCE CHECK checks to ensure that some data has been entered and the value has not been left blank, for example an email address must be given for an online transaction.

&#x1F464; Register &#x1F5D1; Login

(*= Required)

Customer Information

Email*

Screen before login attempt

&#x1F464; Register &#x1F5D1; Login

(*= Required)

Customer Information

Email*

Screen after login attempt

**Figure 9.7** Presence check error message

A CHECK DIGIT is the final digit included in a code; it is calculated from all the other digits in the code. Check digits are used for barcodes, product codes, International Standard Book Numbers (ISBN) and Vehicle Identification Numbers (VIN).

Check digits are used to identify errors in data entry caused by mis-typing or mis-scanning a barcode. They can usually detect the following types of error:

- an incorrect digit entered, for example 5327 entered instead of 5307
- transposition errors where two numbers have changed order, for example 5037 instead of 5307
- omitted or extra digits, for example 537 instead of 5307 or 53107 instead of 5307
- phonetic errors, for example 13, thirteen, instead of 30, thirty.

**Figure 9.8** ISBN 13 code with check digit

An example of a check digit calculation is ISBN 13, where the 13th digit of the ISBN code is calculated using the following algorithm.

1 Add all the odd numbered digits together, excluding the check digit.
2 Add all the even numbered digits together and multiply the result by 3.
3 Add the results from 1 and 2 together and divide by 10.
4 Take the remainder, if it is zero use this value, otherwise subtract the remainder from 10 to find the check digit.

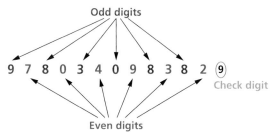

**Figure 9.9** ISBN

Using the ISBN above 9 7 8 0 3 4 0 9 8 3 8 2 without its check digit:

1  9 + 8 + 3 + 0 + 8 + 8 = 36
2  3(7 + 0 + 4 + 9 + 3 + 2) = 75
3  (36 + 75)/10 = 11 remainder 1
4  10 − 1 = 9 the check digit.

To check that an ISBN 13 digit code is correct a similar process is followed.

1  Add all the odd numbered digits together, including the check digit.
2  Add all the even number of digits together and multiply the result by 3.
3  Add the results from 1 and 2 together and divide by 10.
4  The number is correct if the remainder is zero.

Using the ISBN above 9 7 8 0 3 4 0 9 8 3 8 2 9 with its check digit:

1  9 + 8 + 3 + 0 + 8 + 8 + 9 = 45
2  3(7 + 0 + 4 + 9 + 3 + 2) = 75
3  (45 + 75)/10 = 12 remainder 0
4  Remainder is 0 therefore number is correct.

## Activity 9.9

a  Find the check digit for the ISBN 978190612400.
b  Are these ISBNs correct?
   i   9718780171500
   ii  9781234567897

## Activity 9.10

● Find an ISBN, then show that its check digit is correct.
● Working in pairs find two ISBNs each, copy one down with a transposition error and the other one correctly. Swap your ISBNs and see if you can find the one with the error.
● Look at a correct ISBN, can you think of an error that this system will not identify and explain with an example why this is the case?

## Activity 9.11

Find out about the modulo 11 check digit calculation and how it is used for VINs.

## Activity 9.12

Find out how limit checks and consistency checks are used.

## Activity 9.13

Which validation checks could you use for the following? You may decide that more than one validation check is required.

a Entering a telephone number.
b Entering a student's name.
c Entering a part number in the form XXX999, where X must be a letter and 9 must be a digit.

## 9.4.2 Verification

Verification is checking that data has been accurately copied onto the computer or transferred from one part of a computer system to another.

Verification methods include:

- double entry
- screen/visual check
- parity check
- checksum.

For DOUBLE ENTRY the data is entered twice, sometimes by different operators; the computer system compares both entries and outputs an error message requesting that the data is entered again if they are different.

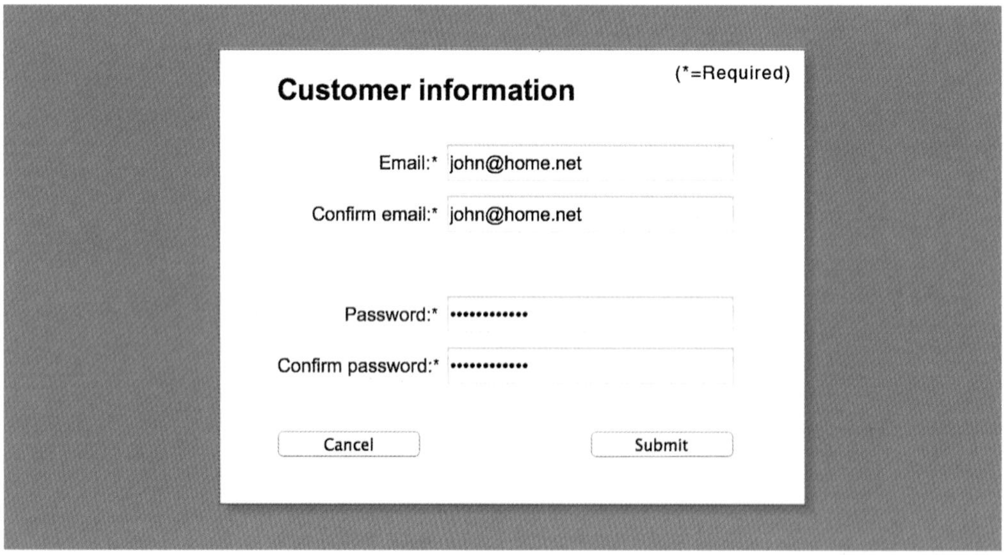

**Customer information** (*=Required)

Email:* john@home.net

Confirm email:* john@home.net

Password:* ••••••••••••

Confirm password:* ••••••••••••

Cancel          Submit

**Figure 9.10** Double entry

A SCREEN/VISUAL CHECK is a manual check completed by the user who is entering the data. When the data entry is complete the data is displayed on the screen and the user is asked to confirm that it is correct before continuing. The user either checks the data on the screen against a paper document that is being used as an input form or confirms from their own knowledge if the data is about them.

Parity checks and checksums are discussed in Sections 2.3.1 and 2.3.3.

## 9.5  Using trace tables

A thorough, structured approach is required to find out the purpose of an algorithm, which involves recording and studying the results from each step in the algorithm. This will require the use of test data and trace tables.

Consider the algorithm represented by the following flowchart:

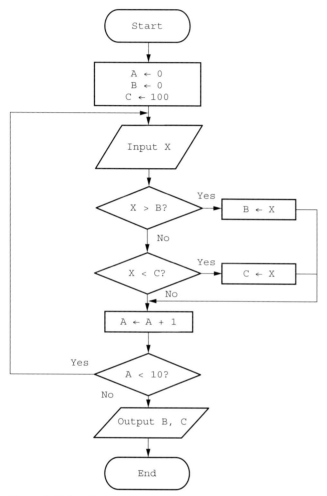

**Figure 9.11** Flowchart to trace

A TRACE TABLE can be used to record the results from each step in an algorithm; it is used to record the value of an item (variable) each time that it changes. This manual exercise is called a DRY RUN. A trace table is set up with a column for each variable and a column for any output. For example:

**Table 9.1** Trace table

| A | B | C | X | Output |
|---|---|---|---|--------|
| 0 | 0 | 100 | | |
| | | | | |
| | | | | |

Test data is then used to dry run the flowchart and record the results on the trace table.

Test data: 9, 7, 3, 12, 6, 4, 15, 2, 8, 5

**Table 9.2** Completed trace table for flowchart

| A | B | C | X | Output |
|---|---|---|---|--------|
| 0 | 0 | 100 | | |
| 1 | 9 | | 9 | |
| 2 | | 7 | 7 | |
| 3 | | 3 | 3 | |
| 4 | 12 | | 12 | |
| 5 | | | 6 | |
| 6 | | | 4 | |
| 7 | 15 | | 15 | |
| 8 | | 2 | 2 | |
| 9 | | | 8 | |
| 10 | | | 5 | |
| | | | | 15 2 |

It can be seen from the output that the algorithm selects the largest and the smallest numbers from a list of 10 positive numbers. The same trace table could have been used if the algorithm had been shown using pseudocode.

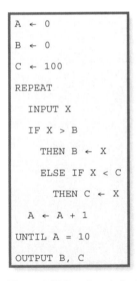

```
A ← 0

B ← 0

C ← 100

REPEAT

    INPUT X

    IF X > B

        THEN B ← X

        ELSE IF X < C

            THEN C ← X

    A ← A + 1

UNTIL A = 10

OUTPUT B, C
```

**Figure 9.12** Pseudocode for the same algorithm to trace

## Activity 9.14

Use the trace table below and the test data 4, 8, 19, 17, 3, 11, 6, 1, 13, 9 to record a dry run of the pseudocode.

**Table 9.3** Trace table to complete for the pseudocode

| A | B | C | X | Output |
|---|---|---|---|--------|
| 0 | 0 | 100 | | |
| | | | | |
| | | | | |
| | | | | |
| | | | | |
| | | | | |
| | | | | |
| | | | | |
| | | | | |
| | | | | |
| | | | | |
| | | | | |

# 9.6    Identifying and correcting errors

## Activity 9.15

Use a trace table and the test data 400, 800, 190, 170, 300, 110, 600, 150, 130, 900 to record another dry run of the pseudocode or flowchart.

Your completed trace table should look like this:

**Table 9.4** Completed trace table

| A | B | C | X | Output |
|----|-----|-----|-----|---------|
| 0 | 0 | 100 | | |
| 1 | 400 | | 400 | |
| 2 | 800 | | 800 | |
| 3 | | | 190 | |
| 4 | | | 170 | |
| 5 | | | 300 | |
| 6 | | | 110 | |
| 7 | | | 600 | |
| 8 | | | 150 | |
| 9 | | | 130 | |
| 10 | 900 | | 900 | |
| | | | | 900 100 |

There is an error as the smallest number has not been identified.

## Activity 9.16

Use a trace table and some negative test data to record another dry run of the pseudocode or flowchart. What error have you found?

The algorithm only works for numbers between 0 and 100; a better algorithm could look like this:

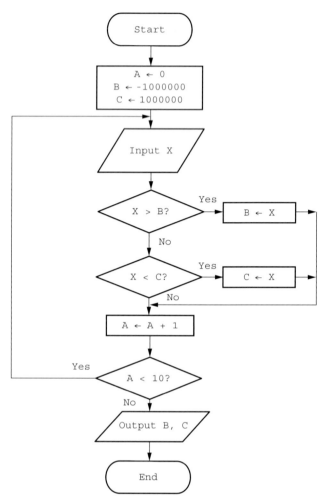

**Figure 9.13** A better algorithm

This algorithm is very similar and works for a much larger range of numbers but it still does not work for every set of numbers. In order to do this the algorithm needs to be rewritten to allow the largest and smallest numbers to be tested against numbers that appear in the list. Figure 9.14 shows this.

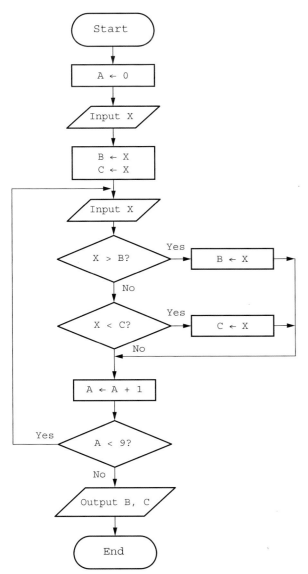

**Figure 9.14** A much better algorithm

**Activity 9.17**
Change the pseudocode so it works for every set of numbers like the flowchart above.

## 9.7  **Producing algorithms**

### 9.7.1 Stages in producing an algorithm

1  Make sure that the problem is clearly specified.
2  Break the problem down into sub-problems; if it is complex, you may want to consider writing an algorithm for each sub-problem. Most problems, even the simplest ones can be divided into:
   - set up
   - input
   - processing
   - output of results.

3 Decide on how any data is to be obtained and stored, what is going to happen to the data and how any results are going to be displayed.

4 Decide on how you are going to construct your algorithm, using a flowchart or pseudocode.

5 Construct your algorithm, making sure that it can be easily read and understood by someone else. This involves setting it out clearly and using meaningful names for any data stores. The algorithms that you have looked at so far in this chapter were not designed with readability in mind because you needed to work out what the problem being solved was.

6 Use several sets of test data (normal, abnormal and boundary) and trace tables to find any errors.

7 If any errors are found, repeat the process until you think that your algorithm works perfectly.

Have a look at a more readable flowchart showing the algorithm to select the largest and smallest numbers from a list of 10 numbers.

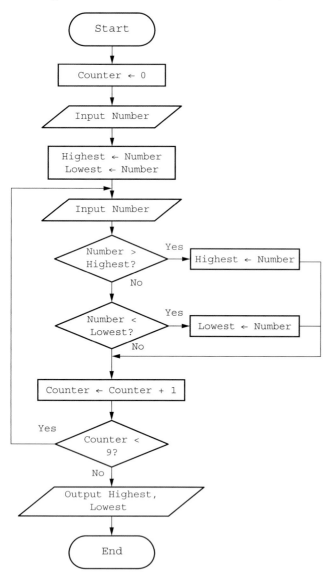

**Figure 9.15** A readable algorithm

More practice on producing algorithms is given in Chapter 10.

## 9.7.2 The effectiveness of a solution

There are many different solutions to the same problem. In order to consider the effectiveness of a given solution ask the following questions.

1 Does the solution work for all sets of data?
2 Does the solution have any unnecessary processes that are never used?
3 Are any actions repeated more often than necessary?
4 Can the solution be simplified and still work as well?

### Activity 9.18

Consider the following algorithm written in pseudocode to check if a child is old enough or tall enough to go on a theme park ride. Comment on its effectiveness.

```
OUTPUT "Please enter age of child in years"

INPUT Age

OUTPUT "Please enter height of child in metres"

INPUT Height

OUTPUT "Please enter weight of child in kilograms"

INPUT Weight

IF Age >= 5 THEN OUTPUT "OK"

IF Height >= 1 THEN OUTPUT "OK"

IF Age < 5 AND Height < 1 THEN OUTPUT "You cannot ride"
```

**Figure 9.16** Pseudocode to check the height and age of a child

# End-of-chapter questions

1 Name and describe the components of a computer system.

2 A computer system is to be developed to provide a modulo 11 check digit for numbers from four to 20 digits in length. Provide a structure diagram for this computer system.

3 A phone app is being developed to split the cost of a restaurant bill between a given number of people. It is being designed to work for up to 12 diners and for bills from $10 to $500.
   a What validation checks should be used for the number of diners and the size of the bill?
   b Provide two sets of normal data and their expected results.
   c Provide some abnormal/erroneous data.
   d Identify the boundary data required and the expected results.

4 Explain what is meant by validation and verification.

5 The following data is to be entered onto an online form:
   • name
   • date of birth
   • password
   • phone number.
   For each item state, with reasons, the validation and verification checks that should be used.

6 Using ISBN 13:
   a Find the check digit for ISBN 978034098382
   b Are these ISBNs correct?
      9780521170653
      9780596158086

7 The following algorithm shown as a flowchart checks the sizes of a consignment of 10 parcels. The dimensions of each parcel are input in centimetres.

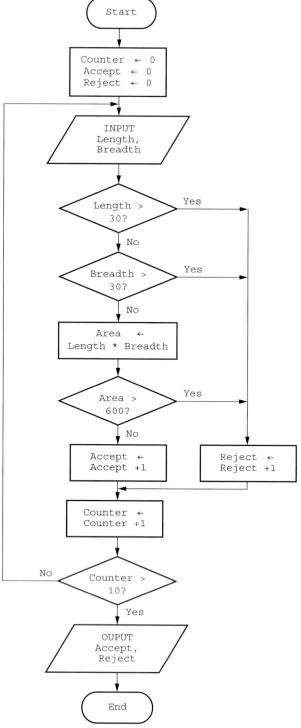

**Figure 9.17** Flowchart

**a** Use this data and the trace table to dry run the algorithm.

15, 10, 20, 17, 32, 10, 30, 35, 30, 15, 30, 28, 25, 25, 20, 15, 40, 20, 12, 10

**Table 9.5** Trace table to complete

| Counter | Length | Breadth | Area | Output |
|---------|--------|---------|------|--------|
|         |        |         |      |        |
|         |        |         |      |        |
|         |        |         |      |        |
|         |        |         |      |        |
|         |        |         |      |        |
|         |        |         |      |        |
|         |        |         |      |        |
|         |        |         |      |        |
|         |        |         |      |        |
|         |        |         |      |        |
|         |        |         |      |        |

**b** What are the rules required to accept a parcel?

**c** Comment on the effectiveness of the algorithm.

**8** This algorithm written in pseudocode adds up 10 positive numbers. It contains several errors.

```
Counter ← 1

FOR Counter ← 1 TO 10

   REPEAT

      PRINT "Enter a positive whole number"

      INPUT Number

   UNTIL Number < 0

   Total ← Total + Counter

   Counter ← Counter + 1

   OUTPUT Total

NEXT
```

**Figure 9.18** Pseudocode for algorithm

**a** Identify all the errors in the algorithm.

**b** Comment on the effectiveness of the algorithm.

**c** Rewrite the algorithm so that it is effective and error free.

**d** Set up a trace table and some test data to dry run your rewritten algorithm.

**e** Identify which items of your test data are normal, erroneous and extreme.

**9** State **two different** validation checks and give an example of their use. Each example should be different. [4]

*Cambridge IGCSE Computer Studies 7010/0420 Paper 12 Q9(b) June 2012*

**10** New software is often developed using top-down (modular) design.

Give **three** benefits of using this method of development. [3]

*Cambridge IGCSE Computer Studies 7010/0420 Paper 13 Q2 November 2012*

**11** A program requires the user to type in a user ID which must be in the form:

XX999999

where X stands for any letter, and 9 stands for any digit.

**a** Name **two** possible validation checks that could be applied to this user ID. [2]

**b** Name a validation check that could **not** be used on this occasion. Give a reason for your choice. [2]

*Cambridge IGCSE Computer Studies 7010/0420 Paper 13 Q5 November 2012*

# 10 Pseudocode and flowcharts

In this chapter you will learn about:

- the pseudocode for assignment, using ←
- the pseudocode for conditional statements
  ```
  IF … THEN … ELSE … ENDIF
  CASE … OF … OTHERWISE … ENDCASE
  ```
- the pseudocode for loop structures
  ```
  FOR … TO … NEXT
  REPEAT … UNTIL
  WHILE … DO … ENDWHILE
  ```
- the pseudocode for input and output statements
  ```
  INPUT and OUTPUT
  (e.g. READ and PRINT)
  ```
- the pseudocode for standard actions
  ```
  totalling (e.g. Sum ← Sum + Number)
  counting (e.g. Count ← Count + 1)
  ```
- the standard flowchart symbols for the above statements, commands and structures.

## 10.1 Introduction

Using pseudocode is a clear and concise way to represent an algorithm. Data items to be processed by the algorithm are given meaningful names in the same way that variables and constants are in a high-level programming language. Pseudocode is not bound by the strict syntax rules of a programming language. It does what its name says; it pretends to be programming code!

To ensure that pseudocode is easily understandable by others it is useful to be consistent in the way that it is written. The pseudocode in this book is written in the following way to help you understand the algorithms more easily:

- Courier New font is used throughout
- all keywords (words used to describe a specific action (e.g. INPUT) are written in capital letters
- all names given to data items and sub-routines start with a capital letter
- where conditional and loop statements are used, repeated or selected statements are indented by two spaces.

## 10.2 Assignment

Values are assigned to an item/variable using the ← operator. The variable on the left of the ← is assigned the value of the expression on the right. The expression on the right can be a single value or several values combined with mathematical operators.

**Table 10.1** Mathematical operators

| Operator | Action |
|----------|--------|
| + | add |
| − | subtract |
| * | multiply |
| / | divide |
| ^ | raise to the power |
| ( ) | group |

Examples of pseudocode assignments:

```
Cost ← 10                        Cost has the value 10
Price ← Cost * 2                 Price has the value 20
Tax ← Price * 0.12               Tax has the value 2.4
SellingPrice ← Price + Tax       SellingPrice has the value 22.4
Gender ← "M"                     Gender has the value M
Chosen ← False                   Chosen has the value False
```

## Activity 10.1

What values will the following variables have after the assignments have been completed?

```
Amount ← 100
TotalPrice ← Amount * 3.5
Discount ← 0.2
FinalPrice ← TotalPrice - TotalPrice * Discount
Name ← "Nikki"
Message ← "Hello" + Name
```

## 10.3 Conditional statements

When different actions are performed by an algorithm according to the values of the variables, conditional statements can be used to decide which action should be taken.

There are two types of conditional statement as shown below with an example of each.

- A condition that can be true or false: IF ... THEN ... ELSE ... ENDIF, for example

```
IF Age < 18
   THEN PRINT "Child"
   ELSE PRINT "Adult"
ENDIF
```

- A choice between several different values: CASE ... OF ... OTHERWISE ... ENDCASE, for example

```
CASE Grade OF
   "A" : PRINT "Excellent"
   "B" : PRINT "Good"
   "C" : PRINT "Average"
   OTHERWISE PRINT "Improvement is needed"
ENDCASE
```

## 10.3.1 IF ... THEN ... ELSE ... ENDIF

For an IF condition the THEN path is followed if the condition is true and the ELSE path is followed if the condition is false. There may or may not be an ELSE path. The end of the statement is shown by ENDIF.

A condition can be set up in different ways:

● Using a Boolean variable that can have the value TRUE or FALSE (see Section 11.4 for details of Boolean variables). For example

```
IF Found
   THEN PRINT "Your search was successful"
   ELSE PRINT "Your search was unsuccessful"
ENDIF
```

● Using comparison operators, as shown in Table 10.2. Comparisons are made from left to right, for example A > B means is A greater than B. Comparisons can be simple or more complicated. For example

```
IF ((Height > 1) OR (Weight > 20) OR (Age > 5)) AND (Age < 70)
   THEN PRINT "You can ride"
   ELSE PRINT "Too small, too young or too old"
ENDIF
```

**Table 10.2** Comparison operators

| Operator | Comparison |
|---|---|
| > | greater than |
| < | less than |
| = | equal |
| >= | greater than or equal |
| <= | less than or equal |
| <> | not equal |
| ( ) | group |
| AND | both |
| OR | either |
| NOT | not |

The algorithm below checks if a percentage mark is valid and a pass or a fail. This makes use of two IF statements. The second IF statement is part of the ELSE path of the first IF statement. This is called a nested IF.

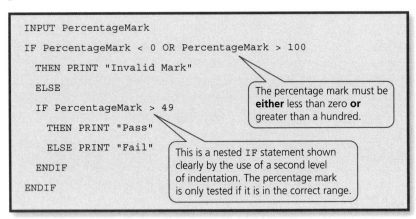

```
INPUT PercentageMark

IF PercentageMark < 0 OR PercentageMark > 100

   THEN PRINT "Invalid Mark"

   ELSE

   IF PercentageMark > 49

      THEN PRINT "Pass"

      ELSE PRINT "Fail"

   ENDIF

ENDIF
```

The percentage mark must be **either** less than zero **or** greater than a hundred.

This is a nested IF statement shown clearly by the use of a second level of indentation. The percentage mark is only tested if it is in the correct range.

**Figure 10.1**

## Activity 10.2

Change the algorithm to check for a mark between 0 and 20 and a pass mark of 10. Decide what normal, boundary and erroneous data you will need to fully test your algorithm.

## 10.3.2 CASE … OF … OTHERWISE … ENDCASE

For a CASE condition the value of the variable decides the path to be taken. Several values are usually specified. OTHERWISE is the path taken for all other values. The end of the statement is shown by ENDCASE.

The algorithm below specifies what happens if the value of Choice is 1, 2, 3 or 4.

```
CASE Choice OF
   1 : Answer ← Num1 + Num2
   2 : Answer ← Num1 - Num2
   3 : Answer ← Num1 * Num2
   4 : Answer ← Num1 / Num2
   OTHERWISE PRINT "Please enter a valid choice"
ENDCASE
```

### Activity 10.3

Use a CASE statement to display the day of the week if the variable DAY has the value 1 to 7 and an error otherwise.

## 10.4 Loop structures

When some actions performed as part of an algorithm need repeating, this is called 'iteration'. Loop structures are used to perform the iteration.

There are three different types of loop structure:

| Operator | Comparison |
|---|---|
| A set number of repetitions | FOR … TO … NEXT |
| A repetition, where the number of repeats is not known, that is completed at least once | REPEAT … UNTIL |
| A repetition, where the number of repeats is not known, that may never be completed | WHILE … DO … ENDWHILE |

**Table 10.3**

All types of loops can perform the same task, for example printing 10 stars.

```
FOR Counter ← 1 TO 10
   PRINT "*"
NEXT
Counter ← 0
REPEAT
   PRINT "*"
   Counter ← Counter + 1
UNTIL Counter > 10
Counter ← 0
WHILE Counter < 10 DO
   PRINT "*"
   Counter ← Counter + 1
ENDWHILE
```

The FOR … TO … NEXT loop is the most efficient for this type of task.

## 10.4.1 FOR ... TO ... NEXT

A variable is set up with a start value and an end value and then incremented in steps of one until the end value is reached and the iteration finishes. The variable can be used within the loop so long as its value is not changed. This type of loop is very useful for reading values into lists.

```
FOR Counter ← 1 TO 10          Counter starts at 1
                               and finishes at 10.
   PRINT "Enter Name of Student"
                               Array (see Chapter 12) items StudentName [1]
   Input StudentName[Counter]  to StudentName [10] have data input.
NEXT
```

**Figure 10.2**

## 10.4.2 REPEAT ... UNTIL

This loop structure is used when the number of repetitions/iterations is not known and the actions are repeated UNTIL a given condition becomes true. The actions in this loop are always completed at least once.

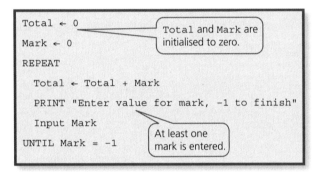

```
Total ← 0          Total and Mark are
                   initialised to zero.
Mark ← 0

REPEAT

   Total ← Total + Mark

   PRINT "Enter value for mark, -1 to finish"

   Input Mark         At least one
UNTIL Mark = -1       mark is entered.
```

**Figure 10.3**

## 10.4.3 WHILE ... DO ... ENDWHILE

This loop structure is used when the number of repetitions/iterations is not known and the actions are only repeated WHILE a given condition is true. If the WHILE condition is untrue when the loop is first entered then the actions in the loop are never performed.

```
Total ← 0            Total initialised to zero.
PRINT "Enter value for mark, -1 to finish"
Input Mark
WHILE Mark <> -1 DO  Condition tested
                     at start of loop.
   Total ← Total + Mark
   PRINT "Enter value for mark, -1 to finish"
   Input Mark
ENDWHILE
```

**Figure 10.4**

**Activity 10.4**
a Write pseudocode to input 10 positive numbers and find the total and the average.
b Write pseudocode to input positive numbers, –1 to finish, and find the total and the average.
c Explain why you chose the loop structures for each task.

## 10.5 Input and output statements

INPUT and OUTPUT are used for the entry of data and display of information. Sometimes READ can be used instead of INPUT; this is usually used for reading from files, which is not covered in this textbook. Frequently PRINT is used instead of OUTPUT.

INPUT is used for data entry. It is usually followed by a variable where the data input is stored, for example:

```
INPUT Name
INPUT StudentMark
```

OUPUT/PRINT is used to display information either on a screen or printed on paper. It is usually followed by a single value that is a string or a variable or a list of values separated by commas, for example:

```
PRINT Name
PRINT "Your name is", Name
OUTPUT Name1, Name2, Name3
```

## 10.6 Standard actions

The ability to repeat actions is very important in the design of algorithms. When an algorithm is turned into a program the same set of actions may be repeated many thousands of times, for example, keeping a running total of the value of goods sold in a supermarket.

```
RunningTotal ← RunningTotal + Value
```

Keeping a count of the number of times an action is performed is another standard action, for example:

```
Count ← Count + 1
```

Counting is also used to count down until a certain value is reached, for example the number of items in stock in a supermarket:

```
NumberInStock ← NumberInStock - 1
```

## 10.7 Examples of algorithms in pseudocode

### Example 1

Tickets are sold for a concert at $20 each. If 10 tickets are bought then the discount is 10%; if 20 tickets are bought the discount is 20%. No more than 25 tickets can be bought in a single transaction.

a Use pseudocode to write an algorithm to calculate the cost of buying a given number of tickets.

b Explain how you would test your algorithm.

a

```
REPEAT
   PRINT "How many tickets would you like to buy?"
   INPUT NumberOfTickets
UNTIL NumberOfTickets > 0 AND NumberOfTickets < 26
IF NumberOfTickets < 10
   THEN Discount ← 0
   ELSE
   IF NumberOfTickets < 20
     THEN Discount ← 0.1
     ELSE Discount ← 0.2
   ENDIF
ENDIF
Cost ← NumberOfTickets * 20 * (1 - Discount)
PRINT "Your tickets cost", Cost
```

b Would use test data with values of

| | |
|---|---|
| 0, 26 | Expected result rejected |
| 1, 25 | Expected results 20, 400 |
| 9, 10 | Expected results 180, 180 |
| 19, 20 | Expected results 342, 320 |

## Activity 10.5

For the test data given in Example 1, identify the type of test data used and suggest some more test data.

# Example 2

A school with 600 students wants to produce some information from the results of the four standard tests in Maths, Science, English and IT. Each test is out of 100 marks. The information output should be the highest, lowest and average mark for each test and the highest, lowest and average mark overall. All the marks need to be input.

a Use pseudocode to write an algorithm to complete this task.

b Explain how you would test your algorithm.

a

```
OverallHighest ← 0
OverallLowest ← 100
OverallTotal ← 0
FOR Test ← 1 TO 4
   SubjectHighest ← 0
   SubjectLowest ← 100
   SubjectTotal ← 0
   CASE Test OF
     1 : SubjectName ← "Maths"
     2 : SubjectName ← "Science"
     3 : SubjectName ← "English"
     4 : SubjectName ← "IT"
     OTHERWISE
   ENDCASE
   FOR StudentNumber ← 1 TO 600
     REPEAT
       PRINT "Enter Student", StudentNumber,"'s mark for ", SubjectName
       INPUT Mark
     UNTIL Mark < 101 AND Mark > -1
     IF Mark < OverallLowest THEN OverallLowest ← Mark
     IF Mark < SubjectLowest THEN SubjectLowest ← Mark
     IF Mark > OverallHighest THEN OverallHighest ← Mark
     IF Mark > SubjectHighest THEN SubjectHighest ← Mark
     OverallTotal ← OverallTotal + Mark
     SubjectTotal ← SubjectTotal + Mark
   NEXT
   SubjectAverage ← SubjectTotal/600
   PRINT SubjectName
   PRINT "Average is ", SubjectAverage
   PRINT "Highest Mark is ", SubjectHighest
   PRINT "Lowest Mark is ", SubjectLowest
NEXT
OverallAverage ← OverallTotal/2400
PRINT "Overall Average is ", OverallAverage
PRINT "Overall Highest Mark is ", OverallHighest
PRINT "Overall Lowest Mark is ", OverallLowest
```

b For the algorithm to be tested by dry running, it would be a good idea to reduce the number of students to 5 and the number of subjects to 2.

## Activity 10.6

a Identify the changes you would need to make to the algorithm for Example 2 to reduce the number of students to 5 and the number of subjects to 2.
b Identify the test data needed to test Example 2 with the reduced number of students and subjects.
c With the set of data you have chosen, set up and complete a trace table so that you can compare your expected results with the actual results when you dry run the algorithm.

## 10.8 Standard flowchart symbols

Flowcharts are drawn using standard symbols.

### 10.8.1 Begin/End

Terminator symbols are used at the beginning and end of each flowchart.

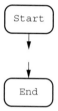

**Figure 10.5** Terminator symbols

### 10.8.2 Process

Process symbols are used to show when values are assigned to an item/variable like an assignment in pseudocode.

**Figure 10.6** Process symbol

### 10.8.3 Input/Output

Input/Output symbols are used show input of data and output of information.

**Figure 10.7** Input/Output symbol

### 10.8.4 Decision

Decision symbols are used to decide which action is to be taken next. These can be used for selection and repetition/iteration.

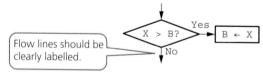

**Figure 10.8** Decision symbol

### 10.8.5 Flow lines

Flow lines are used to show the direction of flow which is usually, but not always, top to bottom and left to right.

**Figure 10.9** Flow line

# Example 1 (continued)

Tickets are sold for a concert at $20 each, if 10 tickets are bought then the discount is 10%, if 20 tickets are bought the discount is 20%. No more than 25 tickets can be bought in a single transaction.

c Draw a flowchart for the algorithm to calculate the cost of buying a given number of tickets.

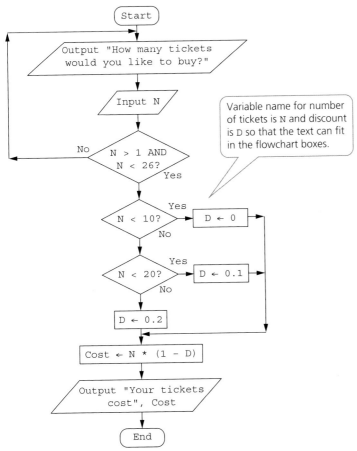

Variable name for number of tickets is N and discount is D so that the text can fit in the flowchart boxes.

**Figure 10.10** Flowchart for Example 1

## Activity 10.7

Draw a flowchart for the algorithm given in Example 2.
Choose the method you think is the clearest way to show this algorithm and explain why it is the clearest.

# End-of-chapter questions

1 Show two ways of selecting different actions using pseudocode.

2 You have been asked to write the pseudocode to choose the correct routine from the menu shown below.

   a Decide which type of conditional statement you are going to use.

   b Explain your choice.

   c Write the pseudocode.

   d Select your test data and explain why you chose each value.

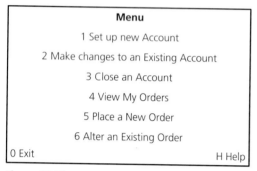

**Menu**

1 Set up new Account

2 Make changes to an Existing Account

3 Close an Account

4 View My Orders

5 Place a New Order

6 Alter an Existing Order

0 Exit                                    H Help

**Figure 10.11**

3 Show **three** ways a loop to add up five numbers and print out the total can be set up using pseudocode. Explain which loop is the most efficient to use.

4 A sweet shop sells 500 different sorts of sweets. Each sort of sweet is identified by a unique four-digit code. All sweets that start with a one (1) are chocolates, all sweets that start with a two (2) are toffees, all sweets that start with a three (3) are jellies and all other sweets are miscellaneous and can start with any other digit except zero.

   a Write an algorithm, using a flowchart, which inputs the four-digit code for all 500 items and outputs the number of chocolates, toffees and jellies.

   b Explain how you would test your flowchart.

   c Decide the test data to use and complete a trace table showing a dry run of your flowchart.

5 The temperature in an apartment must be kept between 18°C and 20°C. If the temperature reaches 22°C then the fan is switched on; if the temperature reaches 16°C then the heater is switched on, otherwise the fan and the heaters are switched off. The following library routines are available:

   • GetTemperature
   • FanOn
   • FanOff
   • HeaterOn
   • HeaterOff

   Write an algorithm, using pseudocode or a flowchart, to keep the temperature at the right level.

6 Daniel lives in Italy and travels to Mexico, India and New Zealand. The time differences are:

| Country | Hours | Minutes |
|---------|-------|---------|
| Mexico | −7 | 0 |
| India | +4 | +30 |
| New Zealand | +11 | 0 |

**Table 10.4**

Thus, if it is 10:15 in Italy it will be 14:45 in India.

   a Write an algorithm, using pseudocode or otherwise, which:

   • inputs the name of the country
   • inputs the time in Italy in hours (H) and minutes (M)
   • calculates the time in the country input using the data from the table
   • outputs the country and the time in hours and minutes. [4]

   b Describe, with examples, **two** sets of test data you would use to test your algorithm. [2]

   *Cambridge IGCSE Computer Studies 7010/0420 Paper 11 Q17 June 2011*

7 A school is doing a check on the heights and weights of all its students. The school has 1000 students. Write an algorithm, using pseudocode or a flowchart, which

   • inputs the height and weight of all 1000 students
   • outputs the average (mean) height and weight
   • includes any necessary error traps for the input of height and weight. [5]

   *Cambridge IGCSE Computer Studies 7010/0420 Paper 11 Q17 November 2010*

8 A small café sells five types of item:
  - bun            0.50 dollars
  - coffee         1.20 dollars
  - cake           1.50 dollars
  - sandwich       2.10 dollars
  - dessert        4.00 dollars

  Write an algorithm, using pseudocode or a program flowchart only, which
  - inputs every item sold during the day
  - uses an item called 'end' to finish the day's input
  - adds up the daily amount taken for each type of item
  - outputs the total takings (for all items added together) at the end of the day
  - outputs the type of item that had the highest takings at the end of the day.      [6]

  *Cambridge IGCSE Computer Studies 7010/0420*
  *Paper 13 Q16 November 2012*

9 5000 numbers are being input which should have either one digit (e.g. 5), two digits (e.g. 36), three digits (e.g. 149) or four digits (e.g. 8567).
  Write an algorithm, using pseudocode or a flowchart only, which
  - inputs 5000 numbers
  - outputs how many numbers had one digit, two digits, three digits and four digits
  - outputs the percentage of numbers which were outside the range.      [6]

  *Cambridge IGCSE Computer Studies 7010/0420*
  *Paper 13 Q15 November 2013*

# 11 Programming concepts

## 11.1 Introduction

Chapters 9 and 10 have enabled you to develop your computational thinking by writing algorithms to perform various tasks. This chapter will show you how to put your computational thinking to the ultimate test by writing computer programs to perform tasks.

So far you have tested your algorithms by dry running. Once you have written a program for your algorithm, and when there are no syntax errors (see Section 7.4.1), you should then use a computer to run the program to complete the task you have specified. The computer will perform the task exactly as you have written it; you may need to make some changes before it works exactly as you intend it to.

## 11.2 Programming

In Chapter 7 you learnt that programs could be written in high- or low-level languages then translated and run. This chapter will introduce you to the programming concepts required for practical use of a high-level language.

There are many high-level programming languages to choose from. For Cambridge IGCSE Computer Science any high-level programming language may be used, however if you plan to continue your studies with A Level Computer Science then one of Visual Basic, Pascal/Delphi or Python is recommended.

Many programming languages are free to download and use. This chapter shows the use of programming and should be used in conjunction with learning the syntax of an appropriate programming language.

Programs developed in this chapter will be illustrated using the following freely available languages:

- Scratch: a good basic introduction to programming for beginners that is freely available from MIT. Scratch makes programming easy and fun to learn as it uses visual building blocks. It is useful as an introduction.
- JavaScript: a scripting language that works in any browser, no download needed. JavaScript works with the HTML (see Section 1.6.2).
- Python: a general purpose, open source programming language that promotes rapid program development and readable code.

The traditional introduction to programming in any language is to display the words 'Hello World' on a computer screen. The programs look very different:

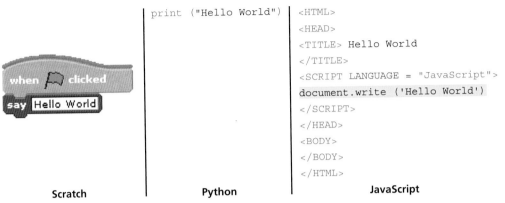

| Scratch | Python | JavaScript |

**Figure 11.1** Programs to display

---

**Activity 11.1**

Have a look at all three programs and decide which program is the easiest to understand.

---

Scratch and Python work in their own Integrated Development Environments (IDEs).

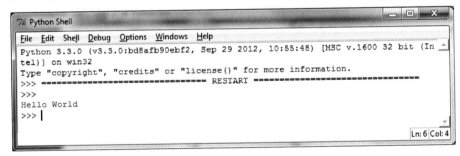

**Figure 11.2** Python IDE

**Figure 11.3** Scratch program running

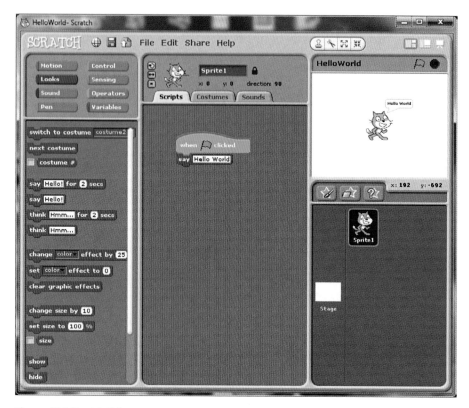

**Figure 11.4** Scratch IDE

JavaScript works in a browser.

**Figure 11.5** JavaScript working in a browser

## Activity 11.2

In the high-level programming language that your school has chosen to use, write and run your own program that displays the words 'Hello Computer Scientists'.

# 11.3 Declaration and use of variables and constants

A VARIABLE in a computer program is a named data store that contains a value that may change during the execution of the program. In order to make programs understandable to others, variables should be given meaningful names.

A CONSTANT in a computer program is a named data store that contains a value that does not change during the execution of the program. In order to make programs understandable to others, constants should be given meaningful names.

Not all programming languages explicitly differentiate between constants and variables but programmers should be clear which data stores can be changed and which cannot be changed. There are several ways of doing this, for example:

- use of capital letters:                          `PI = 3.142`
- meaningful names that begin with Const:  `ConstPi = 3.142`

It is considered good practice to declare at the start of a program the constants and variables to be used in that program. Declarations are expected in programs written for the tasks specified in the IGCSE Computer Science pre-release material (see Section 1.2.3).

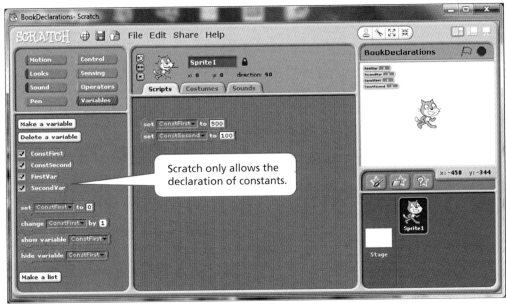

**Figure 11.6** Variable and constant declarations in Scratch

```
var FirstVar, SecondVar;
const ConstFirst = 500, SecondConst = 100;
or
var FirstVar;
var SecondVar;
const ConstFirst = 500;
const ConstSecond = 100;
```

Constants need to be assigned their values when they are declared because they do not change.

**Figure 11.7** Variable and constant declarations in JavaScript

```
FirstVar = 20
SecondVar = 30
ConstFirst = 500
ConstSecond = 100
or
FirstVar, SecondVar = 20, 30
ConstFirst, ConstSecond = 500,100
```

Variables and constants are declared in Python by assigning values.

**Figure 11.8** How to declare variables and constants in Python

**Activity 11.3**

In the high-level programming language that your school has chosen to use, declare the variables and constants you would use in an algorithm to find the volume of a cylinder.

## 11.4 Basic data types

In order for a computer system to process and store data effectively, different kinds of data are formally given different types. This enables:

- data to be stored in an appropriate way, for example, as numbers or characters
- data to be manipulated effectively, for example numbers with mathematical operators and characters with concatenation
- automatic validation in some cases.

### Integer

An INTEGER is a positive or negative whole number that can be used with mathematical operators.

### Real

A REAL NUMBER is a positive or negative number with a fractional part. Real numbers can be used with mathematical operators.

Not all programming languages distinguish between real numbers and integers. JavaScript makes no distinction; Python does with the use of built-in functions.

```
FirstInteger = int(25)      sets up an integer variable with the value of
                            25 in Python
FirstReal = float(25)       sets up a real variable with the value of
                            25.0 in Python
```

### Char

A variable or constant of type CHAR is a single character.

```
var Gender = 'F'                    JavaScript
Gender = 'F' or Gender = "F"   Python
```

### String

A variable or constant of type STRING is several characters in length. Strings vary in length and may even have no characters: an empty string. The characters can be letters and/or digits and/or any other printable symbol. For example:

```
Var TelephoneNumber = '44121654331'  JavaScript
Var FirstName = 'Emma'               JavaScript
Var UnRepeatable = '@!&&@@##!'        JavaScript
TelephoneNumber = '44121654331'      Python
FirstName = 'Emma'                   Python
UnRepeatable = '@!&&@@##!'            Python
```

**Activity 11.4**

In the high-level programming language that your school has chosen to use, write and run your own program that displays the words 'Hello <YourName>'. Use a string variable to store YourName.

**Boolean**

A **Boolean** variable can have only two values: TRUE or FALSE.

```
Var AgeOver21 = true    JavaScript
AgeOver21 = true        Python
```

---

## Activity 11.5

At the start of a program to store some personal information you need to set up variables to store the following data:

- name
- address
- gender
- over/under 18 years of age
- colour of hair
- shoe size
- weight in kilograms.

You also need to set up constants for male and female.

a  Select meaningful variable names and types for your constants and variables.
b  In the high-level programming language that your school has chosen to use, write and run your own program that displays the values you have used to initialise your variables and constants.
c  Make sure that you can input new values and select suitable test data for your program.

---

# 11.5 How to make your program work

Programs work by automatically following one instruction after another in sequence. Look at the following examples.

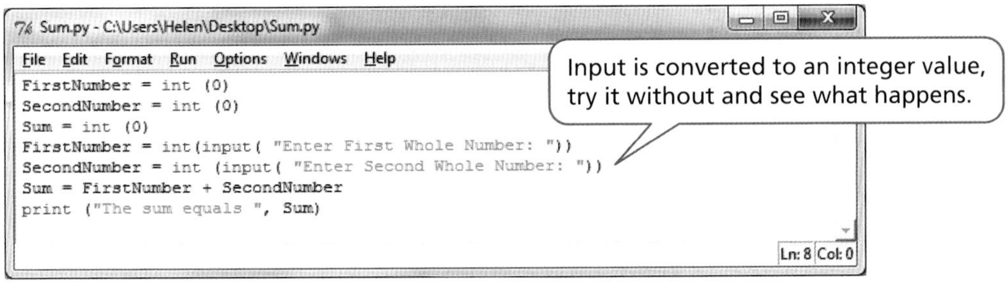

**Figure 11.9** Python program

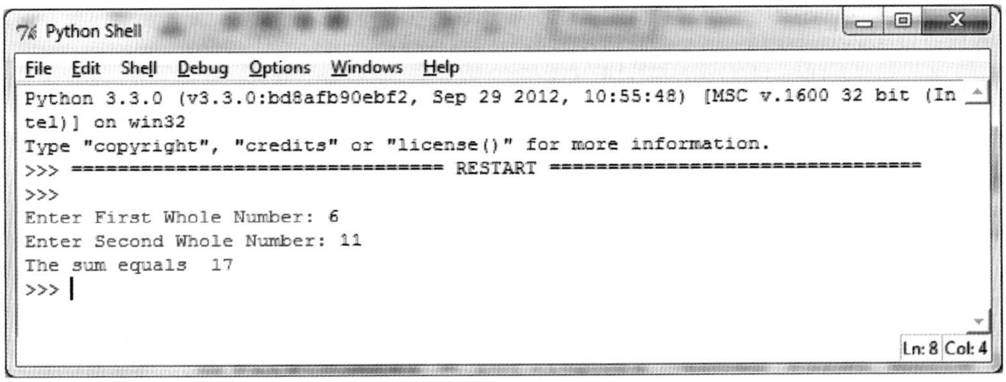

Input is converted to an integer value, try it without and see what happens.

**Figure 11.10** Python program running

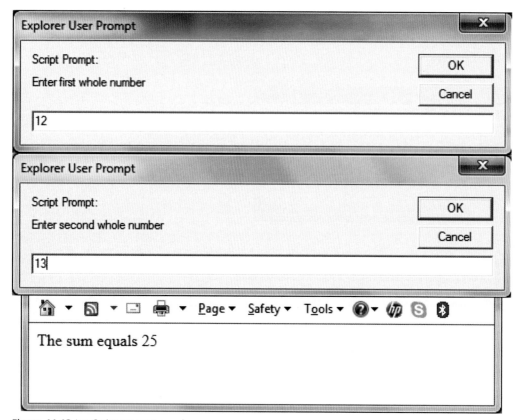

```
C:\Users\Helen\Desktop\Sequence.html - Notepad++

File  Edit  Search  View  Format  Language  Settings  Macro  Run  TextFX  Plugins  Window  ?  X

L McNicholas Standardisation Excercise.dat   Latest business newWorked Example!.html   Latest business ne

 1   <HTML>
 2   <HEAD>
 3   <TITLE> Sequence
 4   </TITLE>
 5   <SCRIPT LANGUAGE = "JavaScript">
 6   var FirstNumber = 0;
 7   var SecondNumber = 0;
 8   var Sum = 0;
 9   FirstNumber = window.prompt('Enter first whole number', '');
10   SecondNumber = window.prompt('Enter second whole number', '');
11   FirstNumber = parseInt (FirstNumber);
12   SecondNumber = parseInt (SecondNumber);
13   Sum = FirstNumber + SecondNumber;
14   document.write('The sum equals ', Sum);
15   </SCRIPT>
16   </HEAD>
17   <BODY>
18   </BODY>
19   </HTML>

nb char : 468       Ln : 7   Col : 13   Sel : 0          Dos\Windows  ANSI          INS
```

Input is converted to an integer value, try it without and see what happens.

**Figure 11.11** JavaScript program

```
Explorer User Prompt                                    X

Script Prompt:                                        OK
Enter first whole number
                                                     Cancel

12
```

```
Explorer User Prompt                                    X

Script Prompt:                                        OK
Enter second whole number
                                                     Cancel

13
```

The sum equals 25

**Figure 11.12** JavaScript program running

Sometimes the next instruction to be obeyed will depend upon what has already happened before and a selection has to take place. Look at the following examples.

```
7% Selection.py - C:\Users\Helen\Desktop\Selection.py
File  Edit  Format  Run  Options  Windows  Help

FirstNumber = int (0)
SecondNumber = int (0)
Sum = int (0)
FirstNumber = int(input( "Enter First Whole Number: "))
SecondNumber = int (input( "Enter Second Whole Number: "))
if FirstNumber > SecondNumber:
        print ("First Whole Number is largest ", FirstNumber)
else:
        print ("Second Whole Number is largest ", SecondNumber)

                                                      Ln: 3 Col: 0
```

**Figure 11.13** Python program showing selection

```
7% Python Shell
File  Edit  Shell  Debug  Options  Windows  Help

Python 3.3.0 (v3.3.0:bd8afb90ebf2, Sep 29 2012, 10:55:48) [MSC v.1600 32 bit (In
tel)] on win32
Type "copyright", "credits" or "license()" for more information.
>>> =============================== RESTART ===============================
>>>
Enter First Whole Number: 7
Enter Second Whole Number: 3
First Whole Number is largest  7
>>>

                                                      Ln: 8 Col: 4
```

**Figure 11.14** Python selection program running

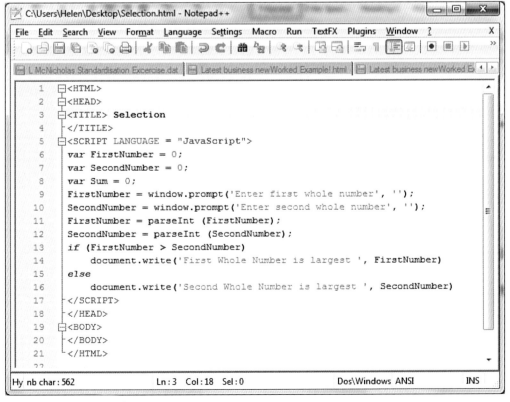

```
C:\Users\Helen\Desktop\Selection.html - Notepad++
File  Edit  Search  View  Format  Language  Settings  Macro  Run  TextFX  Plugins  Window  ?           X

1    <HTML>
2    <HEAD>
3    <TITLE> Selection
4    </TITLE>
5    <SCRIPT LANGUAGE = "JavaScript">
6    var FirstNumber = 0;
7    var SecondNumber = 0;
8    var Sum = 0;
9    FirstNumber = window.prompt('Enter first whole number', '');
10   SecondNumber = window.prompt('Enter second whole number', '');
11   FirstNumber = parseInt (FirstNumber);
12   SecondNumber = parseInt (SecondNumber);
13   if (FirstNumber > SecondNumber)
14      document.write('First Whole Number is largest ', FirstNumber)
15   else
16      document.write('Second Whole Number is largest ', SecondNumber)
17   </SCRIPT>
18   </HEAD>
19   <BODY>
20   </BODY>
21   </HTML>

Hy nb char: 562        Ln: 3  Col: 18  Sel: 0          Dos\Windows ANSI        INS
```

**Figure 11.15** JavaScript selection program

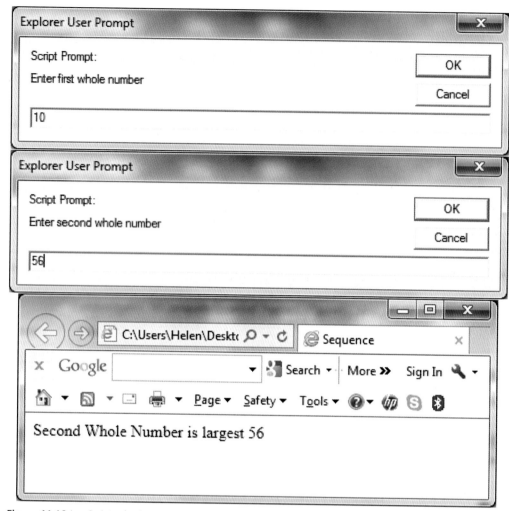

Figure 11.16 JavaScript selection program running

Sometimes instructions need to be repeated several times so a final result can be obtained, this often involves the use of totalling and counting. Look at the following examples.

```
Number = int (0)
Count = int (0)
Sum = int (0)
while Count < 5:
        Number = int(input( "Enter a Whole Number: "))
        Sum = Sum + Number
        Count = Count + 1
print ("Sum of five numbers is ", Sum)
```

Figure 11.17 Python repetition program

**Figure 11.18** Python repetition program running

**Figure 11.19** JavaScript repetition program

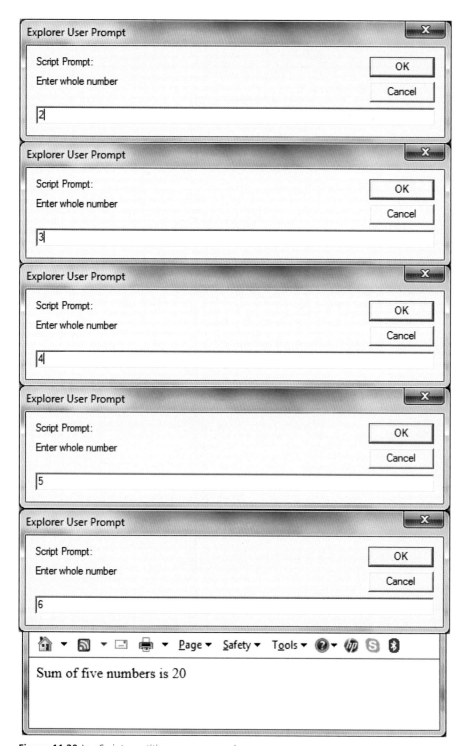

**Figure 11.20** JavaScript repetition program running

## 11.5.1 Sequence

Statements are followed in sequence so the order of the statements in a program is important. Assignment statements rely on the variables used in the expression on the right-hand side of the statement all having been given values. Input statements often provide values for assignment statements. Output statements often use the results from assignment statements.

```
FirstNumber = int(input( 'Enter First Whole Number: '))
SecondNumber = int (input( 'Enter Second Whole Number: '))
Sum = FirstNumber + SecondNumber
print ('The sum equals ', Sum)
```

## 11.5.2 Selection

Selection is a very useful technique, allowing data items to be picked out according to given criteria, for example selecting the largest value or the smallest value, selecting items over a certain price, selecting everyone who is male. This is done with the use of `if` and `case` statements.

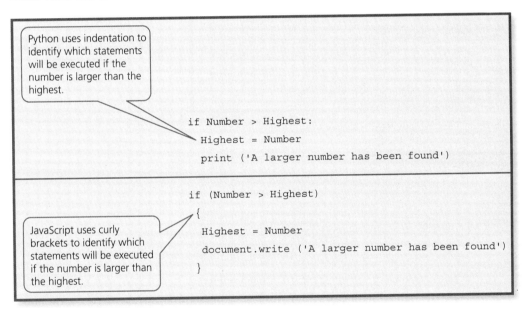

**Figure 11.21** Selection

**Activity 11.6**

Using the high-level programming language that your school has chosen to use, find out about the structure of if...then...else and case statements. Not all programming languages include the use of a case statement.

## 11.5.3 Repetition

Most programming languages support three types of loop:

● a fixed number of repetitions
● an unknown number of repetitions with at least one repetition, as the condition is tested at the end of the loop
● an unknown number of repetitions which may not be completed at all, as the condition is tested at the beginning of the loop.

```
                        for Counter in range (1, 10):
                           print ('*', end = '')
```

Python uses indentation to identify the statements to be executed; an in range statement is used to set up the loop counter.

end = '' keeps all the stars on the same line.

```
for (var Counter = 1; Counter <= 10; Counter = Counter + 1)
   {
     document.write ('*')
   }
```

JavaScript uses curly brackets to identify the statements to be executed; a new variable with a starting value, condition and increment is set up for the loop counter.

**Figure 11.22** Fixed number of repetitions

```
do
  {
    NewValue = window.prompt ('Please enter a positive number', '');
    NewValue = parseFloat (NewValue)
  }
while (NewValue < 0)
```

JavaScript uses curly brackets to identify the statements to be executed; the condition is tested at the end of the loop.

**Figure 11.23** Unknown number of repetitions, at least one completed

```
NewValue = float (input ('Please enter a negative number '))
while NewValue >= 0:
   NewValue = float (input ('Please enter a NEGATIVE number '))
```

Python uses indentation to identify the statements to be executed; the condition is tested at the start of the loop.

```
NewValue = window.prompt ('Please enter a negative number', '');
NewValue = parseFloat (NewValue);
while (NewValue >= 0)
  {
    NewValue = window.prompt ('Please enter a NEGATIVE number', '');
    NewValue = parseFloat (NewValue)
  }
```

JavaScript uses curly brackets to identify the statements to be executed; the condition is tested at the start of the loop.

**Figure 11.24** Unknown number of repetitions, statements in loop may never be used

## 11.5.4 Totalling

Totalling is used with repetition with the total updated every time the loop is repeated. Keeping a running total is one of the most frequently used programming techniques in many computer systems, for example, the total on a receipt at a supermarket checkout.

```
ReceiptTotal = ReceiptTotal + CostOfItem
```

## 11.5.5 Counting

Counting is used with repetition with the counter increased by 1 every time the loop is repeated. Counting items or events is another of the most frequently used programming techniques, for example, counting the number of items sold in a single transaction at a supermarket.

```
NumberOfItems = NumberOfItems + 1
```

As well as counting upwards, a counter can be used to count down with the counter being decreased by 1 every time the loop is repeated, for example, removing an item from stock every time one is sold.

```
NumberInStock = NumberInStock - 1
```

## 11.5.6 Writing programs

### Example 1

Tickets are sold for a concert at $20 each, if 10 tickets are bought then the discount is 10%, if 20 tickets are bought the discount is 20%. No more than 25 tickets can be bought in a single transaction.

a Write a program to calculate the cost of buying a given number of tickets.
b Show how you would test your program.

```
Example1.py - C:\Users\Helen\Desktop\Example1.py

File  Edit  Format  Run  Options  Windows  Help

NumberOfTickets = int (0)
Discount = float (0)
Cost = float(0)
while NumberOfTickets < 1 or NumberOfTickets > 25:
        NumberOfTickets = float(input ('How many tickets would you like to buy? '))
Discount = 0.2
if NumberOfTickets < 10:
        Discount = 0
elif NumberOfTickets < 20:            elif is a combination of
        Discount = 0.1                else and if.
Cost = NumberOfTickets * 20 * (1 - Discount)
print ('Your tickets cost', Cost)

                                                            Ln: 11  Col: 1
```

**Figure 11.25** Example 1 in Python

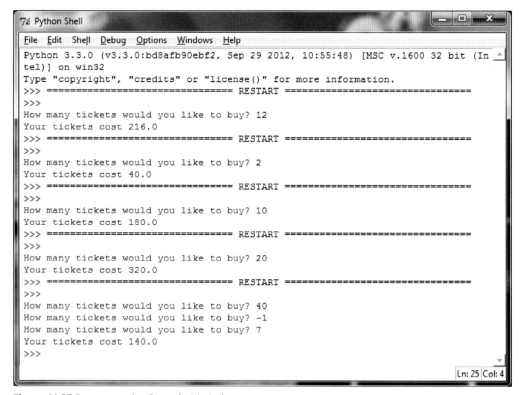

```
1    ☐<HTML>
2    ☐<HEAD>
3    ☐<TITLE> Example 1
4     └</TITLE>
5    ☐<SCRIPT LANGUAGE = "JavaScript">
6     var NumberOfTickets = 0;
7     var Discount = 0.0;
8     var Cost = 0.0;
9     do
10   ☐   {
11        NumberOfTickets = window.prompt('How many tickets would you like to buy? ', '');
12        Number = parseInt (NumberOfTickets);
13   └   }
14    while ((NumberOfTickets < 1 ) || (NumberOfTickets > 26 ));
15    Discount = 0.2;
16    if (NumberOfTickets < 10)
17   ☐   {
18        Discount = 0.0
19   └   }
20    else
21   ☐   {
22           if (NumberOfTickets < 20)
23   ☐      {
24           Discount = 0.1
25   └      }
26   └   }
27    Cost = NumberOfTickets * 20 * (1 - Discount);
28    document.write('Your Tickets cost  ', Cost)
29    └</SCRIPT>
30    └</HEAD>
31   ☐<BODY>
32    └</BODY>
33    └</HTML>
```

|| is OR in JavaScript

**Figure 11.26** JavaScript program for Example 1

```
Python 3.3.0 (v3.3.0:bd8afb90ebf2, Sep 29 2012, 10:55:48) [MSC v.1600 32 bit (In
tel)] on win32
Type "copyright", "credits" or "license()" for more information.
>>> ============================== RESTART ==============================
>>>
How many tickets would you like to buy? 12
Your tickets cost 216.0
>>> ============================== RESTART ==============================
>>>
How many tickets would you like to buy? 2
Your tickets cost 40.0
>>> ============================== RESTART ==============================
>>>
How many tickets would you like to buy? 10
Your tickets cost 180.0
>>> ============================== RESTART ==============================
>>>
How many tickets would you like to buy? 20
Your tickets cost 320.0
>>> ============================== RESTART ==============================
>>>
How many tickets would you like to buy? 40
How many tickets would you like to buy? -1
How many tickets would you like to buy? 7
Your tickets cost 140.0
>>>
```

**Figure 11.27** Program testing Example 1 in Python

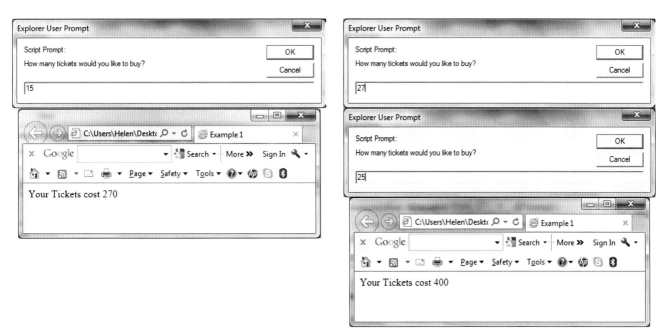

**Figure 11.28** Program testing Example 1 in JavaScript

## Activity 11.7

Using the high-level programming language that your school has chosen to use, write a program for Example 1. Look at the test data used with the Python and JavaScript solutions; explain how you would improve this test data to ensure that your program was fully tested.

## End-of-chapter questions

1 Explain the difference between a variable and a constant in a program.

2 State **four** different basic data types. Illustrate your answer by declaring a variable for each one and assigning it a value.

3 A school with 600 students wants to produce some information from the results of the four standard tests in Maths, Science, English and IT. Each test is out of 100 marks. The information output should be the highest, lowest and average mark for each test and the highest, lowest and average mark overall. All the marks need to be input.

   **a** Write a program to complete this task.

   **b** Explain how you would test your program.

4 Write **three** programs showing the different ways that can be used to add up five numbers and print out the total. Explain which loop is the most efficient to use.

5 A sweet shop sells 500 different sorts of sweets. Each sort of sweet is identified by a unique four-digit code. All sweets that start with a one (1) are chocolates, all sweets that start with a two (2) are toffees, all sweets that start with a three (3) are jellies and all other sweets are miscellaneous and can start with any other digit except zero.

   **a** Write a program, which inputs the four-digit code for all 500 items and outputs the number of chocolates, toffees and jellies.

   **b** Explain how you would test your program.

# 12 Data structures: arrays and using pre-release material

In this chapter you will learn about:

- declaration of one-dimensional arrays
- the use of one-dimensional arrays
- the use of a variable as an index in an array
- reading and writing values in an array using a FOR ... TO ... NEXT loop
- using pre-release material.

## 12.1 Introduction

One of the advantages of using computer systems is their ability to accurately repeat the same tasks many times, for example, producing electricity bills or calculating exam scores. In order to do this, programs are written with loops for repetitions to work with lists of similar items.

These lists are identified by the use of a single name and each item in the list can be found by an index number showing the place in the list. This type of list is called a one-dimensional array. The items in the list are the elements of the array.

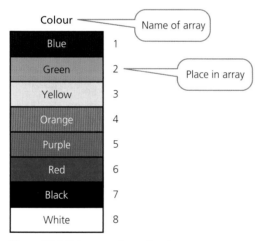

**Figure 12.1** List or one-dimensional array

## 12.2 Arrays

## 12.2.1 One-dimensional arrays

In order to use a one-dimensional array in a computer program, you need to consider:

- what the array is going to be used for, so it can be given a meaningful name
- how many items are going to be stored, so the size of the array can be determined
- what sort of data is to be stored, so that the array can be the appropriate data type.

For example, if a one-dimensional array for all the students' test marks in a class was to be set up:

- array name `StudentMarkTest`
- number of items = number of students in the class, this could be a constant `NoStudents`
- whole numbers need to be stored, data type `Integer`.

Arrays usually start at element 0 or element 1. Often if an array starts at element 0, the size of the array is given as one more than required and element 0 is not used.

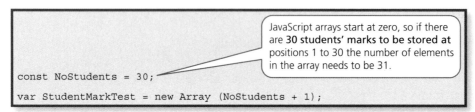

Figure 12.2 Array declaration in JavaScript

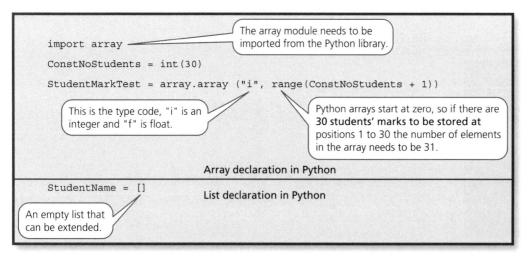

Figure 12.3 Declaration of lists and arrays in Python

## Activity 12.1

Using the high-level programming language that your school has chosen, find out about arrays.

a Is the first element 1 or 0?
b How do you declare the size of an array?
c Can you declare the type of the array?
d Declare an array to store the test marks for a class of 30 students.

## 12.2.2 Using a variable as an index in an array

In order to repeat the same task many times for all the items in a list, each item needs to be referred to in the same way using the index number for each element of the one-dimensional array. If a variable is used for this index number, then the same code can be re-used for each item.

```
StudentMarkTest[Counter]  = int(input("Please Enter Mark "))
                        Python
StudentMarkTest[Counter]  = window.prompt('Please Enter Mark ','');

StudentMarkTest[Counter]  = parseInt(StudentMarkTest[Counter]);
                        JavaScript
```

**Figure 12.4** Using a variable as an index in an array

This allows several arrays to be used together with the same index number to show related information, for example, each student could sit more than one test and the name and gender of the student could also be recorded.

```
StudentName[Counter]  = window.prompt('Enter Student Name ', '');        JavaScript

StudentGender[Counter]  = window.prompt('Enter Student Gender ', '');

StudentMarkTest1[Counter]  = window.prompt('Enter Student Mark for Test 1 ', '');

StudentMarkTest1[Counter]  = parseInt(StudentMarkTest1[Counter]);

StudentMarkTest2[Counter]  = window.prompt('Enter Student Mark for Test 2 ', '');

StudentMarkTest2[Counter]  = parseInt(StudentMarkTest2[Counter]);
```

Same variable used as the index for four different arrays.

```
StudentName.append (input("Please Enter Student Name "))        Python

StudentGender.append (input("Please Enter Student Gender "))

StudentMarkTest1[Counter]  = int(input("Please Enter Mark for Test 1 "))

StudentMarkTest2[Counter]  = int(input("Please Enter Mark for Test 2 "))
```

Same variable used as the index for the two arrays for the numerical values.

Lists are used for the string and character values.

**Figure 12.5** Use of multiple arrays with the same index

## 12.2.3 Read or write values in an array using a FOR ... TO ... NEXT loop

A FOR ... TO ... NEXT loop uses a fixed number of repeats so it is ideal to use with an array, when the number of elements is known, as the loop counter can be used as the array index. For example a FOR ... TO ... NEXT loop could be used to read values into two arrays to store two sets of test marks for a class of 30 students.

```
                                                    In Python, the loop
                                                    counter, range, needs
                                                    to be one more than
                                                    the final value.
ConstNoStudents = int(30)

for Counter in range (1, ConstNoStudents+1):
                                                                    Python
   StudentMarkTest1[Counter] = int(input("Enter Mark for Test 1 "))

   StudentMarkTest2[Counter] = int(input("Enter Mark for Test 2 "))
```

```
                                                                 JavaScript
const NoStudents = 30;

for (var Counter = 1; Counter <= NoStudents; Counter = Counter + 1)

   {

   StudentMarkTest1[Counter]  = window.prompt('Enter Mark for Test 1 ', '');

   StudentMarkTest1[Counter]  = parseInt(StudentMarkTest1[Counter]);

   StudentMarkTest2[Counter]  = window.prompt('Enter Mark for Test 2 ', '');

   StudentMarkTest2[Counter]  = parseInt(StudentMarkTest2[Counter])

      }
```

**Figure 12.6** Reading values into an array

Another FOR ... TO ... NEXT loop could be used to show values in the arrays that store two sets of test marks for a class of 30 students.

```
ConstNoStudents = int(30)
                                                                 Python
for Counter in range (1, ConstNoStudents+1):

   print (StudentMarkTest1 [Counter])

   print (StudentMarkTest2 [Counter])
```

```
for (var Counter = 1; Counter <= NoStudents; Counter = Counter + 1)

   {
                                                                 JavaScript
   document.write (StudentMarkTest1[Counter])

   document.write (StudentMarkTest2[Counter])

   }
```

**Figure 12.7** Outputting values already stored in an array

## Activity 12.2

Using the high-level programming language that your school has chosen, declare arrays to store:

● the names of a class of 30 students
● the gender of each student as M or F
● the marks for two tests for a class of 30 students.

When storing values that are input in any variable or array, validation checks should be used (see Section 9.4.1). For example when inputting the gender for the activity above only M or F should be allowed.

## Activity 12.3

The examples below test for M.

```
StudentGender.append (input("Please Enter Student Gender"))          Python

while StudentGender[Counter] != "M":

        StudentGender[Counter] = (input("Please Enter Student Gender M or F"))
```

```
StudentGender[Counter] = window.prompt('Enter Student Gender', '');   JavaScript

    while (StudentGender[Counter] != 'M')

        {

        StudentGender[Counter] = window.prompt('Enter Student Gender M or F', '')

        }
```

**Figure 12.8** Checking for gender 'M'

Extend your program to test for:

- both M and F in your student gender array
- marks between 0 and 50 for the first test
- marks between 0 and 100 for the second test.

The two previous activities have enabled you to store validated data in four arrays; once this data is stored you can use it to extract useful information. For example you may want to find the students with the highest and lowest mark for each test, the average mark for each test, the average mark overall and the number of male and female students in each class.

You can find a student with the highest mark for test 1 like this:

```
HighestMarkTest1 = int(0)                                             Python

HighestIndexTest1 = int(0)

for Counter in range (1, ConstNoStudents+1):

    if StudentMarkTest1[Counter] > HighestMarkTest1:

        HighestMarkTest1 = StudentMarkTest1[Counter]

        HighestIndexTest1 = Counter
```

```
var HighestMarkTest1 = 0;                                            JavaScript

var HighestIndexTest1 = 0;

for (var Counter = 1; Counter <= NoStudents; Counter = Counter + 1)

    {

        if (StudentMarkTest1[Counter] > HighestMarkTest1)

        {

        HighestMarkTest1 = StudentMarkTest1[Counter];

        HighestIndexTest1 = Counter;

        }

    }
```

**Figure 12.9** Finding the student with the highest mark for test 1

## Activity 12.4

Now extend your program as follows:

a Find the students with the highest marks for tests 1 and 2.

b Find the students with the lowest marks for tests 1 and 2. Hint: set your lowest mark variables to 50 and 100.

c Find the average mark for each test. Hint: use a running total and divide by the number of students at the end.

d Find the number of male and female students. Hint: count either males or females and calculate the other by taking away from 30.

# 12.3 Using pre-release material

In order to answer practical questions based on pre-release material, you will need to practise the skills you have learnt so far. The pre-release material will arrive a few months before your examination; you can discuss it with your teacher and your fellow students.

You need to practise applying your skills to the tasks mentioned in the scenario, which is different for each examination series.

Here is a checklist of useful things to do.

1 Read through the pre-release material several times. Check with your teacher if there is anything at all that you do not understand.

2 For each task, write an algorithm using both pseudocode and a flowchart to show what is required.

3 Choose sets of test data that you will need to use, and work out the expected results. Remember to use normal, boundary and erroneous data. Be able to give reasons for your choice of test data.

4 Complete trace tables to test your pseudocode and flowcharts. This will enable you to ensure that both the pseudocode and the flowcharts work properly. It is a good idea to get another student to trace your algorithms as well.

5 Decide which works best for each task, pseudocode or a flowchart, and why.

6 Before starting to write your program for each task:
   • decide the variables, including any arrays, and constants you will need
   • decide the data types required for these
   • decide the meaningful names you will use
   • be able to explain your decisions.

7 If you are asked to repeat the same thing many times, for example adding up totals, complete the task for one and check it works before repeating it many times.

8 Write and test each task. You can use the same test data as you used for your pseudocode and flowcharts.

## Activity 12.5

Work through the checklist with the pre-release material for your examination.

# 13 Databases

In this chapter you will learn about:
- what databases are used for
- database structure
- practical uses of a database.

## 13.1 Introduction

A DATABASE is a structured collection of data that allows people to extract information in a way that meets their needs. The data can include text, numbers, pictures: anything that can be stored in a computer.

Databases are very useful in preventing data problems occurring because:
- data is only stored once – no data duplication
- if any changes or additions are made it only has to be done once – the data is consistent
- the same data is used by everyone.

## 13.2 What are databases used for?

To store information about people, for example:
- patients in a hospital
- students at a school.

To store information about things, for example:
- cars to be sold
- books in a library.

To store information about events, for example:
- hotel bookings
- results of races.

### Activity 13.1
Find **five** more uses for databases, and for each one decide what sort of information is being stored.

## 13.3 The structure of a database

Inside a database, data is stored in TABLES, which consists of many RECORDS and each record consists of several FIELDS.

| Table | | | | |
|---|---|---|---|---|
| Record 1 | Field 1 | Field 2 | Field 3 | Field 4 |
| Record 2 | Field 1 | Field 2 | Field 3 | Field 4 |
| Record 3 | Field 1 | Field 2 | Field 3 | Field 4 |
| Record 4 | Field 1 | Field 2 | Field 3 | Field 4 |
| Record 5 | Field 1 | Field 2 | Field 3 | Field 4 |
| Record 6 | Field 1 | Field 2 | Field 3 | Field 4 |

**Figure 13.1** Structure of a database table

Tables contain data about one type of item, person or event, for example:

- a table of patients
- a table of books
- a table of doctor's appointments.

Each record within a table contains data about a single item, person or event, for example:

- Winnie Sing (a hospital patient)
- IGCSE Computer Science (a book)
- the 15:45 appointment on 27 January 2014.

Each field contains one specific piece of information about a single item, person or event, for example:

- For a hospital patient the fields could include:
  - first name
  - family name
  - date of admission
  - consultant
  - ward number
  - bed number.
- For a book the fields could include:
  - title
  - author
  - ISBN.

---

### Activity 13.2

What fields would you expect to find in each record for a doctor's appointments?

---

In order to be sure that each record can be found easily and to prevent more than one copy of the same record being kept, each record includes a PRIMARY KEY field. Each primary key field in the table is unique.

| Table | | | | | |
|---|---|---|---|---|---|
| Record 1 | Primary key | Field 1 | Field 2 | Field 3 | Field 4 |
| Record 2 | Primary key | Field 1 | Field 2 | Field 3 | Field 4 |
| Record 3 | Primary key | Field 1 | Field 2 | Field 3 | Field 4 |
| Record 4 | Primary key | Field 1 | Field 2 | Field 3 | Field 4 |
| Record 5 | Primary key | Field 1 | Field 2 | Field 3 | Field 4 |
| Record 6 | Primary key | Field 1 | Field 2 | Field 3 | Field 4 |

**Figure 13.2** Structure of a database table including a primary key

The primary key can be a field that is already used, provided it is unique, for example the ISBN in the book table, or a new field added to each record, for example, a unique hospital number could be added to each hospital patient's record.

Sometimes, a primary key can be formed by using two or more existing fields, for example, the doctor's appointments could have a primary key made from the date and the time of each appointment.

# 13.4 Practical use of a database

As a Cambridge IGCSE Computer Science student you need to be able to do the following:

- define a single-table database from given data storage requirements
- choose a suitable primary key for a database table
- perform a query-by-example from given search criteria.

In order to do this you will need to use a relational database management system. The following case study shows how to set up a database with Microsoft Access and complete the tasks described above.

## Case study

Boys and girls between the ages of seven and eleven can join a cub scout group. (http://en.wikipedia.org/wiki/Cub_Scout)

Each cub scout group needs to keep records about its members. Most groups will keep the following information about each cub in their group:

**Personal Details Form**

To ensure our records are up to date, please fill out all of the information below. Without a completed form, your child will not be able to participate in meetings/activities.

| Personal Details | |
|---|---|
| Name: | |
| Date of Birth: | |
| Address: | |
| Gender: | |
| School: | |
| Telephone Number: | |
| Date Joined: | |

**Figure 13.3** Data collection form

## 13.4.1 Defining a database

This section shows you how to define a single-table database from given data storage requirements and choose a suitable primary key.

To create the cub scout database, open Access, select the Blank database template

**Available Templates**

Home

Blank database    Blank web database    Recent templates    Sample templates    My templates

Office.com Templates                                          Search Office

**Figure 13.4** Blank database

and type the filename CubScout and click the Create button.

**Blank database**

File Name

CubScout

Create

**Figure 13.5** Creating the cub scout database

Select the table design view

File

View

**Figure 13.6** Design View

and name the table Cub.

Save As

Table Name:

Cub

OK          Cancel

**Figure 13.7** Naming the table

Set up the fields to match the data collection form and include the primary key. Each field will require a meaningful name and a data type must be selected. The basic data types were introduced in Section 11.4. They are available in Access but the names are different.

| Computer program | Access |
|---|---|
| Integer | Number/Integer |
| Real | Number |
| Char | Text/field length 1 |
| String | Text |
| Boolean | yes/no |

**Table 13.1**

Access also has other data types that will be useful: Date/Time and Currency.

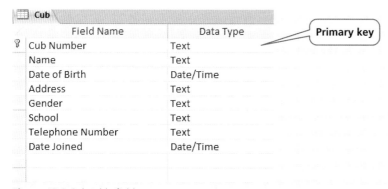

Figure 13.8 Cub table fields

Access allows validation checks to be built in for each field, for example the gender field:

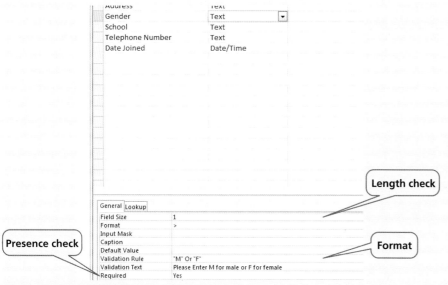

Figure 13.9 Gender field validation

## Activity 13.3
Decide which other fields should be validated.

## 13.4.2 Getting information from a database
This section shows you how to perform a query-by-example (QBE) from given search criteria.

The cub scout leader wants to be reminded before the first meeting in the month of any cub scouts who will have a birthday that month.

To set up a query-by-example to perform this task, open the database CubScout, select the Create tab followed by Query Design.

Figure 13.10

Then add table Cub.

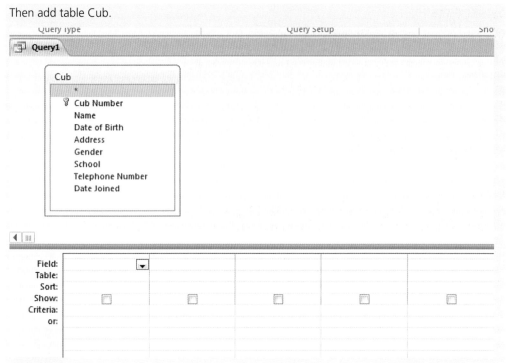

**Figure 13.11**

The cub scout leader wants to see the *Name* of any cub with a *Date of Birth* this month.

Select the fields *Name* and *Date of Birth*, check the box to display the *Name* and check that the month of the *Date of Birth* is the same as the current month.

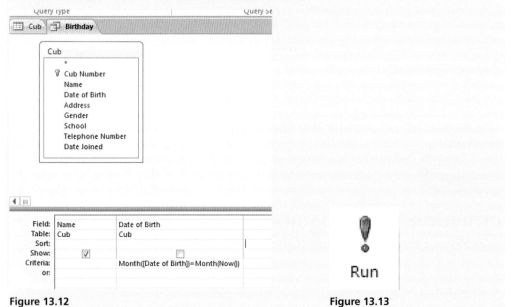

**Figure 13.12**                                             **Figure 13.13**

Then run the query to test it.

## Activity 13.4

Set up a cub scout database with 10 records in it. Include appropriate validation. Using query-by-example, write a query to pick out any cubs born this month.

The cub scout leader wants to put each cub into a group called a 'six'. Each 'six' can have up to six cubs in it and is given a name, for example red, yellow, blue or green. Add a new text field called *Six*, put each cub into a six. Using query-by-example, write a query to pick out any cubs in the red six.

# End-of-chapter questions

1 A database of students is to be set up with the following fields:
   - Family name
   - Other names
   - Student ID
   - Date of birth
   - Date of entry to school
   - Current class
   - Current school year/grade
   - Email address.

   a Select a data type for each field.
   b Which fields should be validated and which fields should be verified?
   c Decide the validation rules for those fields which should be validated.
   d Which field would you choose for the primary key?
   e Choose a suitable format for the student ID.
   f Build a database with at least 10 records. Include all your validation checks. Ensure there are at least three different classes and two different years/grades.
   g Set up and test QBEs to:
      i Print Other names, Family name and Email address in alphabetical order of family name
      ii Select all the students from a given class
      iii Select all the students for a year/grade and print Other names, Family name and Data of birth, grouping the students by class.

**2** A motor car manufacturer offers various combinations of
- seat colours
- seat materials
- car paint colours.

A database was set up to help customers choose which seat and paint combinations were possible.

| code | seat material | | seat colour | car paint colours | | | | | | |
|------|-------|---------|------|-------|-----|-------|------|-------|--------|------|
| | cloth | leather | | white | red | black | blue | green | silver | grey |
| CB | Y | N | black | Y | Y | Y | Y | Y | Y | Y |
| LB | N | Y | black | N | Y | N | N | N | Y | Y |
| CC | Y | N | cream | N | Y | Y | Y | N | N | N |
| LC | N | Y | cream | N | Y | Y | Y | N | N | Y |
| CG | Y | N | grey | N | Y | Y | Y | Y | Y | N |
| LG | N | Y | grey | N | N | N | Y | N | Y | Y |
| CR | Y | N | red | Y | N | Y | N | N | Y | Y |
| LR | N | Y | red | Y | N | Y | N | N | Y | Y |
| CL | Y | N | lime | N | N | N | Y | N | N | N |
| LL | N | Y | lime | N | N | Y | Y | Y | N | N |

*Notes: N = no, not a possible combination, Y = yes, combination is possible.*

**Figure 13.14**

**a** How many records are shown in the database?

**b** The following search condition was entered using a query-by-example grid:

| Field: | cloth | car paint colours | code |
|--------|-------|-------------------|------|
| Table: | seat material | blue | seat material |
| Sort: | | | |
| Show: | ☐ | ☐ | ☑ |
| Criteria: | = 'Y' | = 'Y' | |
| or: | | | |

**Figure 13.15**

What will be displayed?

**c** A customer wants to know the possible combinations for a car with leather seats and either silver or grey paint.

What search condition needs to be input? Copy and complete the table.

| Field: | | | | |
|--------|--|--|--|--|
| Table: | | | | |
| Sort: | | | | |
| Show: | ☐ | ☐ | ☐ | ☐ |
| Criteria: | | | | |
| or: | | | | |

**Figure 13.16**

3 A database was set up to compare oil companies. A section of the database is shown below:

| Code | Name of company | No of employees | No of countries | Head office | Profits (billion $) | Share price ($) |
|------|-----------------|-----------------|-----------------|-------------|---------------------|-----------------|
| AR | Arrows | 60 000 | 30 | Americas | 8.0 | 39.00 |
| GZ | Gazjeti | 35 000 | 4 | Asia | 5.0 | 44.50 |
| KO | Konoco | 40 000 | 22 | Americas | 10.0 | 18.55 |
| OS | Oilbras | 56 000 | 11 | Americas | 4.0 | 59.60 |
| SD | Sand Oil | 102 000 | 51 | Europe | 12.0 | 15.30 |
| SN | Southern Oil | 50 000 | 15 | Americas | 11.0 | 10.90 |
| ST | Static Oil | 80 000 | 31 | Americas | 10.0 | 52.05 |
| SU | Summation | 70 000 | 40 | Europe | 9.0 | 30.40 |
| WP | Wasp Petrol | 90 000 | 44 | Europe | 15.0 | 92.80 |

Figure 13.17

    a How many fields are there in **each** record? [1]

    b The following search condition was entered:

      (**No of countries** < 30) AND (**Head office** = "Americas")

      Using **Code** only, which records would be output? [2]

    c What search condition is needed to find out which oil companies have a share price less than $50 or whose profits were greater than 8 billion dollars? [2]

      *Cambridge IGCSE Computer Studies 7010/0420 Paper 13 Q12 June 2013*

4 A database was set up to keep track of goods in a shop. A section of the database is shown below:

| Item code | Number in stock | Re-order level | Price of item ($) | Value of stock ($) | Items ordered |
|-----------|-----------------|----------------|-------------------|--------------------|---------------|
| 1113 | 155 | 200 | 1.50 | 232.50 | Yes |
| 1124 | 84 | 50 | 2.50 | 210.00 | No |
| 1200 | 30 | 60 | 5.00 | 150.00 | Yes |
| 1422 | 600 | 500 | 1.00 | 600.00 | No |
| 1515 | 90 | 100 | 2.00 | 180.00 | No |
| 1668 | 58 | 50 | 4.00 | 232.00 | No |
| 1801 | 60 | 100 | 8.00 | 480.00 | No |
| 1844 | 195 | 200 | 1.50 | 292.50 | Yes |

Figure 13.18

    a How many records are shown in this section of database? [1]

    b i Using **Item code** only, what would be output if the following search was carried out?

        (**Number in stock** < **Re-order level**) AND (**Items ordered** = "No") [2]

      ii What useful information does this search produce? [1]

    c Write a search condition to locate items costing more than $2.00 or which have a stock value exceeding $300.00. [2]

      *Cambridge IGCSE Computer Studies 7010/0420 Paper 13 Q9 November 2013*

# Index